D0937682

BEST OF

Belgrade

Andrew Stone

How to use this book

Colour-Coding & Maps

Each chapter has a colour code along the banner at the top of the page that is also used for text and symbols on maps (eg all venues reviewed in the Highlights chapter are orange on the maps). The fold-out maps inside the front and back covers are numbered from 1 to 4. All sights and venues in the text have map references; eg, (3, B3) means Map 3, grid reference B3. See p64 for map symbols.

Prices

Multiple prices listed with reviews (eg 50/30DIN) usually indicate adult/concession admission to a venue. Concession prices can include senior, student, member or coupon discounts. Meal cost and room rate categories are listed at the start of the Eating and Sleeping chapters, respectively.

Text Symbols

- ☎ telephone
- ✉ address
- 💻 email/website address
- € admission
- ☽ opening hours
- ⓘ information
- Ⓜ metro
- 🚌 bus
- Ⓟ parking available
- ♿ wheelchair access
- 🍴 on-site/nearby eatery
- 👶 child-friendly venue
- Ⓥ good vegetarian selection

Best of Belgrade
1st edition – Jun 2006

Published by Lonely Planet Publications Pty Ltd
ABN 36 005 607 983

Australia	Head Office, Locked Bag 1, Footscray, Vic 3011
	☎ 03 8379 8000 fax 03 8379 8111
	💻 talk2us@lonelyplanet.com.au
USA	150 Linden St, Oakland, CA 94607
	☎ 510 893 8555 toll free 800 275 8555
	fax 510 893 8572
	💻 info@lonelyplanet.com
UK	72–82 Rosebery Avenue, London EC1R 4RW
	☎ 020 7841 9000 fax 020 7841 9001
	💻 go@lonelyplanet.co.uk

This title was commissioned in Lonely Planet's London office by Fiona Buchan and produced by Cambridge Publishing Management Limited. **Thanks** to Glenn Beanland, David Burnett, Piotr Czajkowski, Brendan Dempsey, Ryan Evans, Fayette Fox, Quentin Frayne, Michala Green, Mark Griffiths, Imogen Hall, Corey Hutchison, Glenn van der Knijff, Anthony Phelan, Charles Rawlings-Way, Jessica Rose, Michael Ruff, Wibowo Rusli, Jacqui Saunders, Fiona Siseman, Ray Thomson, Rachel Wood

Photographs by Lonely Planet Images and Greg Elms except for the following: p13, p15, p23 Photolibrary, p24 Patrick Horton/Lonely Planet Images, p25 agefotostock/Jon Arnold.

Cover photograph The cosy downstairs bar of the Federal Association of Globetrotters, Doug McKinlay/Lonely Planet Images.

All images are copyright of the photographers unless otherwise indicated. Many of the images in this guide are available for licensing from Lonely Planet Images: www .lonelyplanetimages.com.

ISBN 1 74104 859 1

Printed through Colorcraft Ltd, Hong Kong.
Printed in China

Contents

From the Publisher

THE AUTHOR
Andrew Stone

Back in 1988 Andrew staggered for the first time into Croatia and Serbia (back then still parts of Yugoslavia) under the weight of a heavy backpack while on an Inter Railing holiday. It wasn't an electrifying first visit; holiday campsites run by communists are even less fun than they sound. Fortunately, he more than made up for it on his return visit when he got stuck into Belgrade's vibrant nightlife, restaurant, bar and clubbing scene. When not researching and writing guidebooks Andrew works as a freelance business and travel journalist and divides his time between Sydney and London.

Thanks first of all to Vesna, my fellow author and Balkans expert, for all her pretrip help and advice. Thanks too to those who helped me on the ground. They include Slobodan, Nemanya, the staff at the Tourist Organisation of Belgrade and Mina from Yellowcab. Finally, thanks to Igor Brakus for having me on his show and to his listeners on Radio B92 for all their Belgrade tips.

LONELY PLANET AUTHORS

Why is our travel information the best in the world? It's simple: our authors are independent, dedicated travellers. They don't research using just the Internet or phone, and they don't take freebies in exchange for positive coverage. They travel widely, to all the popular spots and off the beaten track. They personally visit thousands of hotels, restaurants, cafés, bars, galleries, palaces, museums and more – and they take pride in getting all the details right, and telling it how it is. For more, see the authors section on **www.lonelyplanet.com**.

PHOTOGRAPHER
Greg Elms

Greg Elms has been a contributor to Lonely Planet for over 15 years, and has completed numerous commissions in that time. The city commissions in particular provide a chaotic mix of search-and-shoot photography in often less than ideal conditions. In Belgrade he was greeted by uniformly grey winter skies which went dark at just 4pm and frequently showered him in snow. He resorted to balancing camera in one hand and umbrella in the other, and for his numb fingers enlisted frequent doses of local *rakija*, or *šljivovica*, or brandy, or whatever was handy.

Introducing Belgrade

Warning: Your first visual impressions when entering this city might tempt you to ask your driver to turn around and take you straight back to the airport. A devastating combination of Nazi bombing and postwar central planning has given once-handsome Belgrade the architectural equivalent of a cauliflower ear and a crooked nose. The city is also, like most of its citizens, a chain smoker, its fume-belching cars and trucks lending the walls of the so-called 'white city' a nicotine patina.

Look beyond the carbuncular concrete, however, and you'll discover compelling reasons to stay. The magnificent and unspoiled Kalemegdan Citadel occupying a sensational position over the Danube, for instance, makes up for every other blighted building on its own. Explore on foot and you'll find a cultured city with a bohemian air, rammed with bookshops and a clutch of interesting museums, galleries and ornate Serbian Orthodox churches.

Spend more than a day here and you'll also realise why Belgrade is a burgeoning party destination. It's not just the ridiculously cheap prices; this is a city with an infectious and irrepressible energy and a populace that's unfailingly friendly, mad about music and up for a big night out. Long after New York has retired to bed with its cup of cocoa, Belgrade is just limbering up. The profusion of bars in town, out of all proportion to its modest GDP, is a wonderful mystery (although a large student population may go some way to explaining it).

There's a party going on in town until late every night of the week; the only trouble is finding it. Many of the best bars and clubs occupy semi-secret locations up obscure alleyways, stairwells or nondescript office blocks. These modern-day speakeasies lend a night out in Belgrade a delicious frisson of secrecy.

Austro-Hungarian splendour on Kneza Mihailova

Neighbourhoods

Most of Belgrade's cultural treasures, not to mention a good share of its restaurants, shops, bars and clubs, lie at your feet in the compact square mile containing **Stari Grad** (Old Town) and the neighbourhood of **Dorćol**. The northwestern edge of Old Town, which ends dramatically where the Sava and Danube Rivers meet, is dominated by the magnificent Kalemegdan Citadel set on a high cliff above the city.

To the southeast of the Citadel and its graceful parkland lies the heart of Stari Grad, along the streets radiating either side of the pedestrianised **Kneza Mihailova**. This leads down to **Trg Republike** (Republic Square) and Belgraders' beloved meeting point – the statue of Prince Michael Obrenović III, liberator of the Serbs from Turkish rule, astride his horse.

OFF THE BEATEN TRACK

In the northwestern area of **New Belgrade** (Novi Beograd) there's a huge swathe of attractive parkland around the Sava and Danube Rivers (Park Prijateljstva, p20).

Zemun (p10) is an elegant town that has become subsumed into Belgrade's outskirts. It has appealing period houses and cottages, old-fashioned open-air produce markets, riverside restaurants and, away from the busy main street, makes a peaceful place to stroll and explore.

In summer you may not escape the crowds on the pretty island of **Ada Ciganlija** (p15), but there's room enough for everyone at this green, water-lapped haven far from the city's smoke and noise.

It is in this part of the city that most of Belgrade's elegant 18th- and 19th-century buildings – survivors of the ravages of several wars – are found. Many are home to museums, restaurants, boutique clothes shops and plenty of bars and cafés. Things get a good deal scruffier, with plenty

Join the throng on Kneza Mihailova

of monolithic concrete buildings and a jam of buses and cars, as you head southeast of Francuska street and south towards the main rail and bus stations.

There are some islands of interest and peace beyond the city centre, however. Further south you ll find the handsome Parliament building and pretty **Tašmajdan Park** and beyond those the towering outline of the church of Sveti Sava, in the district of **Vračar**.

Across the river New Belgrade consists largely of a sprawling mess of run-down high-rise blocks and multilane highways. Along the river, however, you'll find plenty of leafy green space as well as the majority of Belgrade's famous floating nightclub barges.

Itineraries

Belgrade is a large city, but the vast majority of its attractions and diversions lie in the very centre, making it easy and pleasurable to spend most of your time navigating and exploring on foot.

DAY ONE

After a coffee in **Trg Republike**, begin by tackling the **Walking Tour** (p22) to get a feel for the city, taking in **Kalemegdan Citadel** (p8), its museums and its wonderful parkland, and stopping for lunchtime refreshment with a view at **Kalemegdanska Terasa** (p31). Revive with a coffee, juice or cocktail at stylish **Monin** (p37) before heading to **?** (p31) to eat. Head to **Silicon Valley** (p37) for drinks before moving on to **Andergraund** (p38).

DAY TWO

Take the bus or a cab to **Zemun** (p10) for a low-key morning of pottering around Old Town. Enjoy an early lunch by the river at **Aleksandar** (p34). After a coffee back in the city centre and a browse in the

Handsome neo-baroque at Krsmanović House (p19) on Trg Republike

National Museum (p17), whistle for a cab to **Zaplet** (p35) before returning to the centre to seek out **Ben Akiba** (p36).

WORST OF BELGRADE

- Passive smoking. Impossible to avoid. Everyone's a smoker or planning to be one when they grow up.
- Traffic fumes. Thanks to clapped-out Yugos and fume-belching trucks and buses.
- Some ugly, ugly buildings. We have Nazi bombing and subsequent communist Cold War–era central planning to thank for it.

DAY THREE

Head southeast today, first to the **Nikola Tesla Museum** (p12). After a light lunch at **Byblos** (p34) have a walk around towering **Sveti Sava** (p14), perhaps taking in the nearby **Kalenić Pijaca market** (p28). Head back to the centre, kick things off during *aperitivo* hour at the **Movie Bar** (p37) then dine somewhere on **Skadarska** (p33). Finally choose between exploring the **floating nightclubs** (p39) or investigating the mayhem at **Stefan Braun** (p39).

Highlights

KALEMEGDAN CITADEL (1, B2)

Towering high above the confluence of the Danube and Sava Rivers (the city's once-vital military and mercantile arteries), Kalemegdan Citadel is the jewel in Belgrade's otherwise tarnished architectural crown.

It is also a delight to explore. Far from being a forbidding structure, its open layout, dramatic river views, meandering parkland and tree-shaded paths invite the visitor to linger and explore at leisure. It makes for enjoyable people-watching too, since everyone from the youngest to the oldest, the busy and the idle, take time out here.

The Celts raised the first earthworks here and the Romans extended them to secure the settlement of what they called Singidunum. Over the centuries the fortifications were attacked, destroyed and rebuilt as one conqueror removed another. The statistics for this piece of real estate, the key to power in the region, are staggering. Some 115 battles were fought over it; parts of the citadel and the outer city have been razed no fewer than 40 times. Much of what remains today dates from the 18th century, the result of building carried out both by the Austro-Hungarians and the Turks.

Entering the fortifications from Knez Mihailova, a street on the southern side, you will start with the essence of the fortification: the Upper Citadel. The main entrance is **Stambol Gate** (1, B2) built by the Turks around 1750.

Solid as a rock: the entrance to Kalemegdan Citadel

Passing through Stambol Gate you will find yourself surrounded by cannons and tanks. Fear not, it's only the **Military Museum** (p16). Crossing through Clock-Tower Gate, just by the museum, you will see the **Clock Tower** (p19) above, built during the Austrian occupation in the 18th century.

Nearby is the **Great Well** (p19) built by the Austrians from 1721 to 1731 to provide a safe water supply to the fortress. The huge brick shaft, surrounded by a double stairway, is 62m deep and descends 30m underground.

Look up from the well, and you will see the **Victory Monument** (p19), sculpted by Ivan Meštrović in 1928. Beyond the statue is the Sava River and **Veliko Ratno Ostrvo** (The Great War Island), an excellent area for bird-watching.

Another of Meštrović's sculptural legacies is the 1930 **Monument to France** (1, B3), just southeast of the Military Museum. It was erected out of gratitude to the French soldiers who fought and died in Belgrade during WWI.

On the northeastern side is **Despot Gate** (1, B2), the main entrance to the Citadel in medieval times and the best-preserved of the fortifications from that period. The 15th-century **Dizdar Tower** (1, B2), next to the gate, is crowned by the **Astronomical Observatory**, from where you can gaze at the stars (Friday and Saturday nights only).

Nearby is **Dungeon Gate** (1, B2) with two impressive circular towers on each side, used as a prison during medieval times. Just below is the 18th-century **Rose Church of Our Lady** (1, B1). The small but pleasant **City Zoo** (p21) is further down, towards the street.

The battle-scarred **Lower Citadel** (1, A2), closer to the river, is less well-preserved, having suffered heavy destruction in its time. The most impressive of the few sights here is the 15th-century **Nebojša Tower**, built to protect the harbour.

INFORMATION

- ✉ Stari Grad (Old Town)
- € free; observatory 10DIN
- ✕ Kalemegdanska Terasa (p31)

DON'T MISS

- The romantic views from the Victory Monument
- The cannonball holes and shrapnel scars on the huge fortress doors near the Great Well
- An afternoon caffeine kick or a soothing sundowner with the best views in town at the café terrace above Kalemegdanska Terasa (p31)

ZEMUN (2, OFF A1)

Once a separate little town on Belgrade's outskirts, Zemun is now a suburb of the big city. Despite its integration, Zemun has retained its 'town within a city' feel, with a slow pace, and elegant Austro-Hungarian houses lining the narrow streets.

Zemun sits on the south bank of the Danube, some 5km northwest of central Belgrade. This was the southernmost point of the Austro-Hungarian Empire when its opponents, the Turks, were in control of Belgrade. Merchants took advantage of its location between two empires and it became a wealthy little trading enclave.

Today visitors come here to eat or simply to amble along the Danube rather than to trade, although you can still shop at the picturesque **open-air market** and buy locally made textiles.

Walking to Zemun from the city centre is entirely feasible. It takes about an hour and, once you've crossed Branko Bridge (Brankov most), you have a very pleasant walk along the river.

If you don't fancy walking, take a cab from the city centre. Alternatively catch bus 84 from outside Belgrade's central train station and get off in Zemun's main street, Glavna, where the pedestrian-only Lenyinova Street leads down to the Danube.

Stroll by the Danube in elegant Zemun

On Glavna is the **Zemun Museum** (☎ 617 766;, Glavna 9; 100DIN; ◷ 9am-4pm Tue-Fri, 9am-3pm Sat & Sun). It is devoted to the history of Zemun from prehistoric times, and also houses a large collection demonstrating the development of Serbian applied arts.

Above the market area **Grobnjačka**, a narrow cobbled street, leads to remnants of the old village. Beyond, further up the hill towards the **Gardoš**, is a fortress whose origins go back to the 9th century. Fifteenth-century walls remain and, more importantly, the **Tower of Sibinjanin Janko**.

INFORMATION
✉ Zemun suburb
🚌 84
🍴 Aleksandar (p34)

Built in 1896 to celebrate the millennial anniversary of the Hungarian state and to keep an eye on the Turks, the tower guards the city like a misplaced lighthouse. Its base is sadly dilapidated and rubbish is strewn all around but it still makes a terrific viewpoint back across to Kalemegdan

There are great views of the city from the Tower of Sibinjanin Janko

and the city centre. Behind the tower is a peaceful, immaculately kept churchyard and cemetery.

Down the stairs that descend from the tower is **Nikolajevska Church** (Njegoševa 43), an Orthodox church dating back to 1731. Inside this high-vaulted building, and gleaming out of the gloom, is an astoundingly beautiful iconostasis (wall of icons) carved in the baroque style, gold-plated on black and with rows of saints painted on golden backgrounds.

After exploring Old Town, a good way to finish off is at one of the riverside **fish restaurants** (pp34, 35). Most offer a good selection of mainly freshwater-fish, often accompanied by music and, if your throat is up to it, the local *šljivovica* (plum brandy). If you don't want your day to end there, try one of the floating **nightclub barges** nearby (p39).

ZEMUN'S CRIMINAL CONNECTIONS

If you had a mind to scratch beneath Zemun's picturesque exterior, you'd probably discover a lot of dodgy goings-on. This is the stamping ground of the Zemun Clan, one of the most notorious mafia-style groups in the country (implicated in the murder of Prime Minister Zoran Đinđić). A great deal of the redevelopment going on in the district is said to be funded by money laundered from protection rackets and various other nefarious activities. But don't be alarmed, all this criminal activity remains firmly underground.

NIKOLA TESLA MUSEUM (3, E5)

Easily the most inspiring, involving and interesting museum in town, the Nikola Tesla Museum is also a fitting tribute to Nikola Tesla, an inventor who more than earned his right to be placed in the pantheon of great inventors, yet who died in poverty and relative obscurity.

Tesla was the man who electrified the world: he discovered the rotating magnetic field and pioneered the production and distribution of electrical energy based on alternate currents. In other words he invented motors, generators and power-generating turbines, and without him we'd still be using a wind-up mechanism to start our cars. His work on high-frequency oscillations blazed a trail for technological breakthroughs that led to the development of radio communications. In fact, he even pre-empted Marconi's discovery of wireless transmissions.

Tesla's life history is thoroughly, almost obsessively, documented in the first room of the museum (it's also where you'll find an urn containing his ashes) but it is the explanations of his inventions and experiments and the vivid, hands-on demonstrations of his fascinating discoveries that have the most appeal.

INFORMATION

- ☎ 433 886
- ⌨ www.tesla-museum.org
- ✉ Krunska 51
- € 50DIN
- ☯ 10am-noon & 4-8pm Tue-Fri, 10am-1pm Sat & Sun
- 🚌 10

There's archive footage of some of his high-voltage innovations, generating arcs of electrical flame, together with some of the actual devices he created. There are motors demonstrating the application of rotating magnetic fields, the model of his first radio-controlled boat and a display on Tesla's prescient attempts to build 'the world's radio station' (which he hoped would transmit news, music as well as photographs but which he never had the resources to develop). Perhaps most fun is the device that generates noisy sparks and lights a cableless neon lamp you hold in your hand. It's all wonderfully retro 1930s sci-fi B-movie stuff. Even for those who have no comprehension of science, this is a great interactive experience, making the museum a great place to take inquisitive children.

Many, although not all, the displays are subtitled in English as well as Serbian. The museum also offers a slim guide in English offering more background on specific innovations and experiments.

NIKOLA TESLA: AN ELECTRIC LIFE

Nikola Tesla should be as famous as the greats of the modern industrial era such as Albert Einstein, Thomas Edison and Isambard Kingdom Brunel, but somewhere along the way he lost the public relations battle with posterity. It could be argued that Tesla was more than a match for all of the above since he had the talents of all three; he was not only a scientist of genius but a ceaseless innovator and an accomplished engineer.

Born in northern Serbia in 1856, Tesla studied at Graz and Prague universities before moving to Paris in 1882 to work for Edison's Continental Company, where he made the prototype of the induction motor. Two years later he moved to New York, where he began to experiment with X-rays and wireless power transmission.

His invention of the neon light tube changed the look of America's streets forever. He was also responsible for devising a way of transmitting electricity over long distances: those large power stations and towers, attached to cables stretching for miles across many a country's landscape, are all thanks to Nikola Tesla.

He also experimented with remote controls and electric motor ignition, both of which are integral to the modern world, and was a pioneer of radio astronomy. But his more idiosyncratic inventions, like the 'electric laxative', somehow never became household names.

During the height of his career in America, Tesla's fame paralleled that of any other inventor, his name a byword for innovation and almost magical technical achievements. After demonstrating wireless communication in 1893 and winning the 'War of the Currents', he was widely respected as America's greatest electrical engineer.

Yet, despite the fact that much of his early work pioneered modern electrical engineering and many of his discoveries were of groundbreaking importance, in his later years Tesla came to be regarded as an eccentric, even mad, scientist. Never a savvy businessman, he died in New York in 1943, impoverished and all but forgotten. Fittingly, science has posthumously recognised his genius by placing him in the pantheon of greats who have natural forces named after them, such as Faraday and Volta (a Tesla, if you really must know, being a unit of magnetic induction).

It's electrifying: an early AC motor at the Nikola Tesla Museum

SVETI SAVA (2, D4)

It may still be one giant building site, but the as-yet-unfinished church of Sveti Sava is well worth a visit.

Built on the spot where the Turks reputedly burnt the relics of St Sava, the youngest son of a 12th-century ruler, and founder of the independent Serbian Orthodox Church, it is a lengthy work in progress.

Despite the ongoing building work, during work hours visitors are usually free to enter the massive interior and crane their necks to admire the grand dome high above. It's easy to see what the time and effort are going

INFORMATION

✉ Bulevar Stankovića, near Slavija square, Vračar suburb

🚌 Slavija

into inside Sveti Sava, where stone-masons laboriously hand-carve the massive marble friezes that will adorn the acres of space inside the domed interior.

In front of the church is a statue of Serbia's former ruler, the legendary Karađorđe, which in turn is surrounded by Karađorđe park, a pleasant enough space in which to sit, relax and take in the sheer scale of the building.

Sveti Sava still has the builders in after 100 years

A CENTURY IN THE MAKING

Plans to build the church of Sveti Sava were put together as early as 1894, although the final architectural design was not chosen until 1926. The bombing of Belgrade by Germany during WWII delayed things badly as the city devoted its postwar energies to more pressing reconstruction efforts. Work on the church resumed in the late 1980s, only to be halted soon after by the outbreak of civil war. Since then the pace of building has picked up markedly and the church's exterior is now complete. Dedication is said to be just a couple of years away (although no-one's holding their breath).

ADA CIGANLIJA (2, OFF A5)

A wooded island park on the Sava River just southwest of the city centre, between New Belgrade and the suburb of Čukarica, Ada Ciganlija is Belgrade's summer retreat.

It's the perfect haven to escape the heat, crowded streets and ubiquitous traffic fumes of the city and a great place to stroll, cycle or swim. The island is criss-crossed with pathways through appealing woodland and there are several long stretches of beach perfect for picnicking and sunbathing.

INFORMATION
✉ Čukarica suburb
🚌 53, 56
✗ Guštimora (p35)

The lake is very popular with all Belgraders, including its naturists (you can bare all with them 1km upstream of the main swimming area). Adrenaline junkies might like to try the bungee jumping or the water-ski tow. There's also minigolf and boat hire and in summer free outdoor concerts sometimes take place.

Plenty of places overlooking the lake sell refreshments and there are a couple of restaurants on the island. But if you want a great meal after you've swum, lazed and generally explored the island, we recommend trying the seafood at nearby **Guštimora** (p35).

DID YOU KNOW?

The name Ada Ciganlija is thought to be Celtic in origin, and is derived from the word for island *(singa)* and a word describing swampy or submerged land *(lia)*.

Escape to the green haven of Ada Ciganlija

Sights & Activities

MUSEUMS & GALLERIES

Ethnographic Museum (3, C2)
Serbia's bygone agrarian and folk cultures are done colourful and comprehensive justice in this museum packed with displays detailing the many elaborate styles of traditional regional costumes, and documenting Serbian rural life in centuries past. Highlights include the elaborate 19th-century bridal costume with a 'Smiljevac' hat (on the ground floor) and the Montenegrin men's costumes.
☎ 328 1888 ✉ Studentski Trg 13 € 60DIN ☼ 10am-5pm Tue-Sat, 9am-2pm Sun 🚌 Studentski Trg

Historical Museum of Serbia (2, B6)
Also known as Prince Miloš Mansion (who built the park and house the museum occupies), this museum is not in fact dedicated to all of Serbia's history but concentrates in particular on documenting the 1804 revolt against Turkish rule. Look out for the huge, ancient plane tree propped up out front.
☎ 660 422 ✉ Topčider Park ☼ 10am-5pm Tue-Sun

Maršal Tito's grave (2, C5)
If you ever wanted to know what dictators keep in their attics, visit the House of Flowers, the final resting place of Josip Broz Tito (p46) and home to the gifts from fellow presidents and toadying diplomats during his life. Weapons were clearly *de rigueur* tokens of affection between despots and include ornate mother of pearl rifles and all manner of assorted stabbing and maiming devices. Tito's impressive marble grave itself occupies some lovely grounds dotted with statues mythologising events from the great man's life.
☎ 367 1485 ✉ House of Flowers, Bulevar Mira € free ☼ 9am-5pm Tue-Sun Jun-Sep, to 3pm rest of year 🚌 3, 40, 41

Military Museum (1, B3)
A large complex presenting a complete, if rather pedestrian, military history of the former Yugoslavia. Exhibits include weapons captured from the Kosovo Liberation Army (KLA) and from NATO special forces 'terrorists'. Outside are a number of bombs and missiles contributed from the air by NATO in 1999 and a line-up of old guns and tanks. The displays are labelled in Serbian but you can buy an accompanying booklet in English.
☎ 334 4408 ✉ Kalemegdan Citadel € 20DIN ☼ 10am-5pm Tue-Sun

Museum of Contemporary Art (2, B2)
This light, spacious gallery may or may not be showing all of its excellent permanent collection as the curators were changing things at the time of writing. The collection covers three main periods: impressionist (1900–18); expressionist, constructivist and surrealist (1918–41); neosurrealist, modern and contemporary (1945 to present day). Notable artists to look out for include surrealist Marko Ristić, Frano Šimunović

Marble and mythology: Tito's grave

and Petar Dobrović. The temporary exhibitions gallery has retrospectives of Serbian and foreign artists.

☎ 311 5713 ⊠ Muzej Savremene Umetnosti, Novi Beograd € 80DIN ☼ 10am-5pm Mon, Wed, Fri & Sat, noon-8pm Thu, 10am-2pm Sun 🚌 15, 84, 704E, 706

Museum of the Serbian Orthodox Church (3, B3)

A surprisingly diverting ecclesiastical history of the Serbian Orthodox Church. Among the highlights are valuable items such as the robes of King Milutin (13th and 14th century), Ivan The Terrible's cup and various icons, prints and engravings.

☎ 328 2593 ⊠ Kralja Petra 5 € 50DIN ☼ 8am-3pm Mon-Fri 🚊 2, 11, 13

National Museum (3, C3)

This offers the richest museum experience in Belgrade, if all its floors are open when you visit. At the time of writing the excellent lower two floors dedicated to prehistory and early Serbian art and culture

Elegant Ottoman style in the Greeting Room at the Palace of Princess Ljubica

were closed indefinitely for reconstruction. The modern-art gallery on the 3rd floor displays a fraction of its large and impressive collection of national and European art, including work by Rubens, Renoir, Picasso and Monet. Nadežda Petrović (1873–1915), one of Serbia's first female artists, is well represented.

☎ 624 322 ⊠ Trg Republike € 200DIN, free Sun ☼ 10am-5pm Tue,

Wed & Fri, noon-8pm Thu, 10am-2pm Sat & Sun 🚌 Trg Republike

Palace of Princess Ljubica (3, B3)

This 1831 compound is a Balkan-style palace built for the wife of Prince Miloš. The spacious rooms are filled with period furniture. There's also a little hammam (Turkish bath) where Ljubica would have had steams and massages.

☎ 638 264 ⊠ Kneza Sime Markovića 8 € 50DIN ☼ 10am-5pm Tue-Fri, 10am-4pm Sat & Sun

Yugoslav Aeronautical Museum (2, off A3)

This large and impressive museum, located at the airport, displays some rare planes, including a Hurricane, Spitfire and Messerschmitt from WWII, bits of cruise missiles and that infamous American stealth fighter that

BOMBED-OUT BELGRADE

When NATO began bombing Serbia in 1999 (see p46) Belgrade's military, security and intelligence headquarters right in the centre of the city were key targets. Racked by bombs delivered by stealth bombers flying high above, the damage to these still largely **derelict buildings** (3, C5; ⊠ cnr Nemanjina & Kneza Miloša 🚌 41) was massive. You can still see the entry points of the bombs and the great chunks of reinforced concrete the explosions tore from these huge structures. It's a darkly impressive sight.

air defences downed in 1999. Beware, you may be offered the chance to buy a tiny piece of its 'wing' but its provenance is distinctly dodgy.

☎ 670 992 ✉ Suračin € 300DIN ☎ 9am-2pm Tue-Sun Nov-Apr, 9am-7pm Tue-Sun May-Oct 🚌 airport bus

Yugoslav Film Library Theatre (3, D3)

A huge library of more than 82,000 films, stills, books and film magazines, all illustrating the technical development of film throughout the years. It also shows classic films and prints a monthly programme of upcoming screenings (see Entertainment, p40).

☎ 324 8250 🖵 www. kinoteka.org.yu ✉ Kosovska 11 € 🕑 11am-7pm Tue-Sat 🚋 Trg Republike

PLACES OF WORSHIP

Bayrakli Mosque (3, C1)

Belgrade was once a city of slender minarets but today this is its only surviving mosque. Even this modest, rather run-down place of worship, dating back to 1690, was nearly pulled down by an angry mob in March 2004 protesting against anti-Serb pogroms in Kosovo. It remains under police guard today.

✉ cnr Kralja Petra & Gospodar Jevremova 🕑 by appointment only 🚌 Studentski Trg

Saborna Church (3, B2)

To the right of the Palace of Princess Ljubica is

Towering pillars and glittering saints in Serbian Orthodox Sveti Marko Church

Belgrade's 19th-century Orthodox cathedral, a mixture of late baroque and neoclassical styles. Although it is not as grand as some churches, its atmospheric interior is well worth a look, particularly for its fine iconostasis (wall of icons). It remains an important church to Serbs because it holds the tombs of Prince Miloš Obrenović and his two sons and because Vuk Karadžić, the man responsible for phoneticising the Serbian language, is buried in the church's graveyard.

✉ cnr Kralja Petra & Kneza Sime Markovica 🚋 2, 11, 13

Sveti Marko Church (3, E4)

Behind the post office,

this grandiose five-domed church with a bell tower above the main entrance is based on the design of the venerated Gračanica monastery in Kosovo. The church contains the grave of Emperor Dušan (1308–55). Behind it is the tiny white Russian Church with blue domes, erected by Russian refugees who fled the October Revolution of 1917.

☎ 323 1940 ✉ Bulevar Kralja Aleksandra 17 🚌 26, 27

BUILDINGS & MONUMENTS

Burial Chamber of Sheik Mustafa (3, C2)

Little more than a pile of

stones, this is the 18th-century tomb of Sheik Mustafa, a dervish sheik from Baghdad.
✉ cnr Bracé Jugovića & Višnjićeva 🚌 Studentski Trg

Clock Tower (1, B2)
This handsome late 18th-century Turkish baroque clock tower offers some good views from the top, although they are not as good as those from the Victory Monument.

VICTORY MONUMENT

Depicting a male warrior in the buff, the striking **Victory Monument** (1, A2; ✉ Kalemegdan Citadel 🚌 2, 11, 13) by the sculptor Ivan Meštrović, was originally built to stand in the city centre but was moved to Kalemegdan Citadel in the face of prudish complaints about its frontal nudity. It may have been sited here for reasons of delicacy, but that has probably turned out to be a better idea anyway. It's a fantastic location for such a dramatic monument. The statue holds a falcon in one hand – the symbol of Slav freedom – and a sword in the other, representing the defence of peace.

Mind your head if you do decide to clamber around its cramped interior.
✉ Kalemegdan Citadel
€ 50DIN ⏲ 9am-6pm
🚌 2, 11, 13

Gallery of Frescoes (3, B2)
A good place to come if you're interested in Serbian religious art, filled with lovingly re-created full-size replicas (and some originals) of paintings from churches and monasteries around the country. Some fascinating Roman floor mosaics are being reconstructed and can be seen under their protective sheets.
☎ 621 491 ✉ Cara Uroša 20 € 50DIN ⏲ 10am-5pm Mon, Tue & Thu-Sat, 10am-2pm Sun

Great Well (1, A2)
Also known as the Roman Well (although the Romans had nothing to do with its construction), this huge, deep, brick-lined hole in the ground was built in the first half of the 18th century. The shaft and two staircases, up which water was laboriously carried, descend more than 60m, but visitors can explore only the top end of the well.

Krsmanović House (3, C4)
This handsome if modest neo-baroque house (not open to the public) on busy Terazije is where the Kingdom of Serbs, Croats and Slovenes was first pronounced in 1918, a unification that would some years later lead to the federation of Yugoslavia.
✉ Terazije 34 🚌 Trg Republike

ESCAPE FROM THE CITY

Serbia has some wonderful wilderness areas to explore. One of them is **Avala** (2, off C6), a mountain wilderness 16km south of Belgrade and a popular summer destination for Belgraders. It's a beautiful area, replete with water springs and hiking opportunities. There are also the striking WWI and WWII monuments, the most famous being ubiquitous Ivan Meštrović's Monument to the Unknown Hero.

Mausoleum of Damad Ali-Pasha (1, B2)

One of the few remaining Turkish structures still standing on the citadel grounds, this is the tomb of the great Turkish military commander killed at the Battle of Petrovardin in 1716.
⊠ Kalemegdan Citadel
🚋 2, 11, 13

Monument to France (1, B3)

Another work by the celebrated sculptor Ivan Meštrović, the monument was dedicated in 1930 to the French soldiers who died fighting in Yugoslavia in WWI.
⊠ Kalemegdan Citadel
🚋 2, 11, 13

Parliament Building (3, D4)

Not generally open to visitors, this building was the focus of furious anti-Milošević rallies and running battles with the security services in October 2000. TV screens around the world were filled with crowds of people storming this very building.
⊠ Bulevar Kralja Aleksandra
🚌 27

GREEN SPACES & PUBLIC PARKS

Jevremovac Botanical Gardens (3, E3)

This small botanical garden won't break any records for exoticism or for the variety of any particular species (there are only 250 shrub and tree species), but it is a serene space to relax and maybe picnic in.
☎ 768 857 ⊠ 29 Novembra ⏱ 9am-7pm May-Nov 🚌 35, 43, 96

Park Prijateljstva (2, B2)

This huge expanse of lawn and scrubby woodland makes a great walking and running space. The riverside path hugging its northeastern edge takes in all the floating Sava and Danube nightclub barges and runs up as far as the Hotel Jugoslavia, from where it's possible to stroll on to Zemun (p10).
⊠ Novi Beograd (New Belgrade) 🚌 84 🅿

Tašmajdan Park (3, D-E4)

This much-needed green space in a very busy part of town makes an appealing refuge from all the traffic and bustle. Look out for the monuments commemorating those killed during the NATO bombings (p46).
⊠ Bulevar Kralja Aleksandra
⏱ 24hr ♿ fair

Topčider Park (2, B6)
This pleasant park in a gentle valley with a river winding through it offers a couple of interesting monuments, including the Historical Museum of Serbia (p16) and the elegant St Peter and St Paul Church.
✉ Rakovicki Put ◷ 24hr
🚉 Žel. Stanica Topčider

QUIRKY BELGRADE

Museum of Automobiles (3, D3)
A surprisingly large and impressive private collection of cars and motorcycles, including an 1897 motorised trike and a Ford Model T. Choice for our garage

would be the '57 Cadillac convertible: only 25,000km and one careful owner – President Tito.
☎ 334 2625 ✉ Majke Jevrosime 30 € 50DIN
◷ 10am-noon, 6-9pm Tue-Sun

Museum of FC Crvena Zvezda (2, D6)
Strictly for football anoraks only, the museum of Belgrade's premier football club right next to Red Star's ground proudly displays all the club's silverware and photos of its mullet-headed heroes down the years.
☎ 322 4412 ✉ Ljutice Bogdana 1
◷ Mon-Sat 10am-2pm
🚌 47, 48

Railway Museum (3, B5)
Tracing the history of Serbia's railways since the 1850s, this is really only one for groups of train buffs. It's located inside the railway station complex and only opens to organised groups. You can, however, see a couple of fine old locomotives parked in front of the station at any time.
☎ 361 0334
✉ Central Station
◷ weekends only by appointment
€ free
🚌 Central Bus Station

BELGRADE FOR CHILDREN

City Zoo (1, C1)
This small zoo in the grounds of Kalemegdan Citadel is home to hippos, elephants, camels, tigers and other creatures. Smaller visitors should enjoy the excursions around the animal enclosures aboard mini carriages towed by tiny Shetland ponies.
✉ Kalemegdan Citadel grounds € 300DIN
◷ 8am-8pm

Zamak 'Fort' (2, off A1)
A rather incongruous sight along the banks of the Danube just north of the Hotel Jugoslavia, this wooden stockade looks like the film set from a cowboy movie. In fact it's a children's playground, which should keep younger children entertained for a while.
☎ 063 722 5522 ✉ Kej Oslobondenja ◷ 1pm-8pm Mon-Fri, 10am-9pm Sat & Sun 🚌 84 🅿 ♿ fair

Colourful cassowary at Belgrade's City Zoo

Trips & Tours

WALKING TOUR
Belgrade's Historic Highlights

Start your walk beneath the statue of the horseman in **Trg Republike** (Republic Square) and amble up pedestrianised Kneza Mihailova and then left down Kralja Petra to **Saborna Church** (**1**; p18) for a peep inside its atmospheric interior.

Cross the road and continue, turning left into Kneza Sime Markovića for the 19th-century **Palace of Princess Ljubica** (**2**; p17).

Head back up Kneza Sime Markovića to the edge of the park and Kalemedgan Citadel, entering the park opposite the French Embassy and walking along its western edge past the **Great Well** (**3**; p19) and up the stairs to the **Victory Monument** (**4**; p19) for those magnificent views.

Now head up the rest of the hill and ascend the **Clock Tower** (**5**; p19) and then take the short stroll up to the dragon's hoard of weaponry at the **Military Museum** (**6**; p16).

Leave the citadel complex via the outer Stambol Gate and cross the road and tram tracks to join Uzun Mirkova, turning left into Cara Uroša for the **Gallery of Frescoes** (**7**; p19). Return to Uzun Mirkova and continue down to the **Ethnographic Museum** (**8**; p16).

Inspirational art at the Gallery of Frescoes (p19)

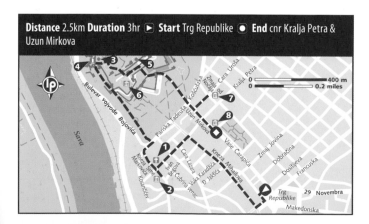

Distance 2.5km **Duration** 3hr ▶ **Start** Trg Republike ● **End** cnr Kralja Petra & Uzun Mirkova

DAY TRIPS
Novi Sad (4, B2)

This pleasing historic town, Serbia's second-largest, has many charms but one big attraction: the Petrovardian Citadel. Towering over the Danube far below and Novi Sad across the bridge, it was built to protect this Austro-Hungarian town from Turkish invasion. There's an engaging little museum, a planetarium and a series of artists' workshops where you can haggle for a piece of local art. The Clock Tower offers some of the best vantage points. The citadel is also the venue for the Exit music festival (www.exitfest.org), an increasingly hip summer gathering, which attracts thousands of partygoers and some big name bands (the White Stripes, Underworld, Fatboy Slim and many top European house DJs have all played here). Back across the river (and past the half-submerged bridges bombed by NATO in 1999, not to mention the local oil refinery), the town centre itself, bustling with commerce and students from the large unversity, is well worth spending some time in. The centre of gravity is Trg Slobode, the spacious but busy town square, which is home to several interesting sights and a tempting array of cafés, restaurants and bars. At the southern end of the square is the ornate City Hall building; in the middle lies the towering, cathedral-size Roman Catholic church of St Mary; and at the northern edge is the Orthodox cathedral of St George, a 19th-century replica of the 17th-century church that burnt down, along with much else of the city centre, during a revolt by a garrison of Hungarian troops in 1848. Dunavska, a picturesque street lined with period houses, leads off the northeastern edge of the square. Also here is the Museum of Foreign Art, which contains mostly Eastern European art dating back as far as the Renaissance. Another worthwhile stop for art is the Gallery of Matica Srpska (at Trg Galleria 1), devoted to Serbian artists of the 17th to the 20th centuries.

INFORMATION

70km northwest of Belgrade

🚌 half-hourly buses link Belgrade's bus station with Novi Sad's, next door to the train station

🚆 almost hourly trains link Belgrade's main station with Novi Sad's train station. Take a taxi (but not from the pirates immediately in front of the station building).

🚗 follow the E75 highway northwest out of Belgrade and take the first exit into Novi Sad

ℹ Tourist Office (☎ 421 811; www.novisadtourism.org.yu; Mihajla Pupina 9; ⏰ 9am-8pm Mon-Fri, 9am-2pm Sat)

Novi Sad's elegant town square

Smederevo (4, C3)

If you still haven't visited enough fortresses, head to Smederevo; this triangular fort with 25 towers and a moat is a humdinger. Overlooking a smallish, otherwise unremarkable industrial town of 40,000 people, the fortress guards the southern bank of the Danube and is a hugely romantic ruin, although it was not so for the many hands that built it.

INFORMATION

46km southwest of Belgrade

- 🚌 A frequent bus service (130DIN, 1½hr) from Belgrade's Lasta bus station makes this a pleasant day trip
- 🚗 Head southeast out of town, on the road hugging the river
- € Fort free; Smederevo Museum 10DIN
- ☾ Fort daylight hr; Smederevo Museum 10am-5pm Mon-Fri, 10am-3pm Sat & Sun

The fortress was built by despot Đurađ Branković in an attempt to halt the advance of the Turks and was constructed in a year. Though completed with vast amounts of forced labour, it's an impressive achievement given the size of the building. Smederevo served as Branković's capital from 1428 to 1430 and did act as a stronghold against the Turks, who finally secured its surrender in 1459. During this era no serious destruction was ever visited upon its walls in battle and the fortress would probably be in near-pristine condition today were it not for some Allied bombing and the massive explosion of a nearby ammunition train in WWII. The fortress is thought to stand on the site of the much earlier Roman settlement of Mons Aureus, and legend has it that its vineyards were planted by the Roman emperor Probus. When Branković became lord of Tokaj, in Hungary, he planted vines from Smederevo on his estates there and from these came the famous white wine, Tokay. Although the nearby town is not that inspiring, there are a couple of sights worth visiting, namely the early 15th-century church, with some colourful 17th-century frescoes, and the Smederevo Museum, which documents the town's history with artefacts dating from Roman times and some interesting frescoes. The centre of Smederevo is compact and easy to navigate. Most of its shops and restaurants are clustered around the main square.

A commanding view of the Danube from Smederevo Fort

ORGANISED TOURS

The **Tourist Organisation of Belgrade** (p57) runs and takes bookings for many of the bus, boat and guided walking tours listed below.

Belgrade Bus Tour

There's no hop-on, hop-off tourist bus service in Belgrade, but reaching all the main central sights is easily done on foot. On Sundays, however, a **tour bus** (3, D4; Nikola Pašic Trg) sets off at 10am for a 90-minute tour of the city.
✉ Nikola Pašic Trg 12
€ 200DIN ☼ 10am

National Guide Association of Serbia

This organisation can arrange independent and licensed guides for city tours on various themes.
☎ 323 5910 ▯ www.utvs.org.yu

The Romantic Express

This steam-hauled train with rather grand period carriages heads to the Austro-Hungarian winemaking town of Sremski Karlovci. Bookings are through **KSR Beograd Tours** (3, C4/5).
☎ 641 258 ✉ KSR Beograd Tours, Milovana Milovanovića 5 ☼ 6.30am-8pm

Royal Compound Tours

These tours of the royal palace compound should be booked beforehand through the tourist information centre. The **tour bus** (3, D4; Nikola Pašic Trg) also leaves

Rest your legs and see the city from the river

from Nikola Pašic Trg.
✉ Nikola Pašic Trg 12
☼ 10.30am-1.30pm Sat & Sun Apr-Oct

Sava & Danube Boat Tours (2, off A1)

Pleasant 90-minute excursions with commentary, exploring the river system around the city by boat. Phone ahead to confirm the trip is running; if they can't make minimum numbers the organisers have been known to cancel tours at the last minute.

☎ 635 622 ✉ Hotel Jugoslavia pier € 200DIN ☼ 6pm Tue-Fri, 4 & 6pm Sat & Sun Apr-mid-Oct.

Wine Tour

Tastings and tours of the vineyards and surrounding wine country on the gently rolling slopes of Mt Fruška Gora around Sremski Karlovci. The tour, which can be booked through the Tourist Organisation of Belgrade (p57), also takes in the 17th-century Grgteg Monastery.

Shopping

Belgrade's not Milan, yet for such a relatively small and modestly wealthy city it offers a surprisingly varied array of clothing for all budgets and styles as well as a good range of local crafts and souvenirs.

The main shopping area lies in Old Town, mainly along pedestrianised Kneza Mihailova, a street lined with department stores and some familiar Western names such as Diesel, Mango, Zara and Benetton. The Serbs must have a collective shoe fetish; everywhere you walk, there are countless shoe shops selling elegant but inexpensive footwear.

Lace table mats, hand-knitted woollens and those multi-billion-dinar banknotes from Serbia's hyper-inflation era are all on sale from stallholders in Kalemegdan Park.

All around the city there is a plethora of street stalls selling newspapers and many a 'genuine' bargain Louis Vuitton bag or Versace top. Cheap pirated CDs and DVDs also abound.

CASH, CARDS & CURRENCY

Shoppers wishing to pay for goods with credit or debit cards should find that most large stores in Belgrade accept them. Needless to say, street stalls, markets and independent outlets almost always deal only in cash, usually in dinars. Quite a few will accept euros as well although you'll need to be careful about the exchange rate you're quoted. A few of the high-end clothing boutiques tend to give prices in euros, although most take dinars if push comes to shove.

CLOTHING & SHOE SIZES

Women's Clothing
Aust/UK	8	10	12	14	16	18
Europe	36	38	40	42	44	46
Japan	5	7	9	11	13	15
USA	6	8	10	12	14	16

Women's Shoes
Aust/USA	5	6	7	8	9	10
Europe	35	36	37	38	39	40
France only	35	36	38	39	40	42
Japan	22	23	24	25	26	27
UK	3½	4½	5½	6½	7½	8½

Men's Clothing
Aust	92	96	100	104	108	112
Europe	46	48	50	52	54	56

Japan	S	M	M		L	
UK/USA	35	36	37	38	39	40

Men's Shirts (Collar Sizes)
Aust/Japan	38	39	40	41	42	43
Europe	38	39	40	41	42	43
UK/USA	15	15½	16	16½	17	17½

Men's Shoes
Aust/UK	7	8	9	10	11	12
Europe	41	42	43	44½	46	47
Japan	26	27	27.5	28	29	30
USA	7½	8½	9½	10½	11½	12½

Measurements approximate only; try before you buy.

CLOTHING

Posher fashion boutiques cluster on or around the middle section of Kralja Petra. The really cutting-edge, locally made threads from up and coming designers lie in less obvious, less expensive locations: many are well worth seeking out.

It may be a trek to get to but there are scores of outlets for several high-end international brands for both men and women over in New Belgrade, inside the **Sava Centre building** (p40) on Milentija Popovića. **The Hyatt Regency** (p43) also has several upscale (mainly men's) clothes outlets, including concessions from Nautica and Zegna.

Department Stores

Millennium Centre (3, C3)
Not so much a department store as a collection of posh boutiques and international label concessions in a covered mall, this is well worth a wander if you're after up-to-the-minute threads. The choice is not quite as wide as at the Sava Centre in New Belgrade, however.
✉ Obilicev venac 16/ Kneza Mihailova 🕙 9am-8pm
🚊 Trg Republike

Yugoexport (3, C3)
A good place to go for inexpensive but good-quality trousers and tops you could wear out of an evening. The basement also sells CDs.
✉ Terazije 🕙 9am-8pm Mon-Sat, 11am-6pm Sun
🚊 Trg Republike

Local Designers

Dragana Ognjenović (3, B2)
Classic eveningwear, dresses and jackets in any colour as long as it's black from this fêted Belgrade fashionista. The elegant tailoring and superb-quality fabrics make up for the limited palette and prices up to 22,000DIN.
☎ 328 5799 🖳 www.draganaognjenovic.com
✉ Kneza sime Markovića 10
🕙 10am-6pm 🚋 2, 11, 13

Identity (3, C2)
Glamorous, sometimes outrageous women's wear popular with local celebrities and TV folk that might include *cheongsam*-style jackets and velvet or silk party skirts, many of them one-offs at around €100 or less. Lots of quirky hats and shoes too.
☎ 328 4044 🖳 identity@eunet.yu ✉ Zmaj Jovina 30 🕙 9am-9pm Mon-Fri, 10am-4pm Sat 🚊 Trg Republike

Lily Tailor (3, E3)
There's a new 'collection' of 10–15 pieces every week

and a couture service with a three-day turnaround for both evening and daywear from these highly respected and capable Belgrade designers. The silk, chiffon, cotton and velvet are sourced from Italy and prices range from €80-€300. Call ahead to check this hard-to-find place is open.
☎ 322 3676 ✉ Koste Stojanovica 6 🕙 by appointment 🚊 Trg Republike 🅿

Milan St Marković (3, D2)
A celebrated designer from an aristocratic Serbian family, Marković makes classic made-to-measure eveningwear, elegantly tailored jackets and luxurious lingerie. The showroom is in a fine classical mansion. Call ahead to check it's open.
☎ 334 1362 🖳 www.milanmarkovic.com
✉ Francuska 🕙 by appointment 🚊 Trg Republike

Schlitz (3, E3)
Schlitz (or 'zipper') is a magpie's nest of wildly

Bright lights and high fashion on Kneza Mihailova

varying men's and women's clothing from 30 of Belgrade's best young designers. The stock includes bags, boots, shoes, shirts and tops, and the defining adjectives are urban, chic, inventive and fun.

☎ 323 6429 ✉ Palmotićeva 23 ☻ 10am-6pm ☒ Trg Republike Ⓟ

Software (3, C4)
A small but smart collection of relatively inexpensive

women's and men's wear including skirts, shirts, clutch bags and scarves in good-quality fabrics and muted colours.
☎ 323 9187 ✉ Terazije 29 ☻ 9am-6.30pm ☒ Trg Republike

BELGRADE MARKETS

Belgrade has several markets worth exploring whether you're after food, memorabilia, cheap threads or just the drama of a big bustle of stalls. There are also several super-markets around Belgrade.

- **Kalenić Pijaca** (2, E4; ✉ Southern end of Njegoševa ☻ mornings daily ☒ Slavija) This sprawling, ramshackle and hugely atmospheric open-air market is at its best on Saturdays and is worth pottering around just for the sheer theatre of it. Country-dwellers descend on this spot to sell every imaginable bit of produce from their farms, including huge wagon wheels of cheese, big fat haunches of ham, long links of cured sausage, locally distilled hooch, bushels of garlic, herbs, spices, flowers, fruit and vegetables. There's also a flower market and a bric-a-brac section where you can haggle for antique oddities and communist-era memorabilia.
- **Craft street market** (3, D5; ✉ cnr Kralja Milana & Njegoševa ☻ 8am-5pm Mon-Sat ☒ Trg Republike) Just south of the city centre, this is a good hunting ground for handcrafted jewellery, original oil paintings and more haberdashery than you can shake a knitting needle at.
- **Zeleni Venac** (Green Wreath market; 3, C3; between Birjuzova, Prisrenka & Brankova bus stops) A place of trade since the 19th century, this covered market has unusual, almost Chinese-style roofs on its chequerboard towers. The rest of the market area is covered with a patchwork of tin, wood and textile, to keep out the sun. Unfortunately, it seems also to have the effect of keeping the smell in. If your airline loses your luggage, fret not: you can stock up on anything here, from cheap clothes to toiletries, dodgy DVDs and, of course, food. This is also a starting and ending point for many of the city buses, including those to Zemun and Ada Ciganlija.
- **Fruit & veg market** (3, C3; ✉ cnr Brankova Prizrenska & Narodnog Fronta; ☻ 6am-1pm) If you don't fancy the trek out to Kalenić Pijaca (see above) and just want to stock up centrally on fresh supplies, head to Belgrade's main fresh produce market, a good hunting ground for fruit, veg and picnic fare.

Verica Rokačević (3, B2)
Sumptuous, one-off, high-end, take-no-prisoners couture is what Verica Rokačević, Belgrade's fashion *grande dame,* is all about. Fabulous eveningwear and dresses for that gallery opening in a dazzling array of textures and fabrics (silk, cashmere, velvet, lace) and patterns. Prices range from 10,000DIN–30,000DIN.
☎ 322 8756 🖳 www.vrcompany.com ✉ Terazije 3, VI Sprat 🕙 10am-6pm 🚊 Studentski Trg

Lingerie
Women'sSecret (3, C3)
Walking into this Spanish chain's store is like entering a Pop Art gallery shortly after a bomb has gone off. Think candy store colours, cartoon designs, a playful aesthetic and reasonable prices. Great for comfortable lingerie, tops, skirts and accessories.
☎ 262 3744 ✉ Kolarceva 6-8 🕙 10am-8pm 🚊 Trg Republike

DESIGN & HOMEWARES

d.o. home (3, B2)
A small, chic, pricey selection of portable homewares including plates, cups, candle holders, ashtrays and napkins from clothes designer Dragana Ognjenović, next door to her boutique.
☎ 328 3939 ✉ Kneza Sime Markovica 10 🕙 10am-6pm 🚊 2, 11, 13

Marokana (3, E3)
As the name implies, this interiors shop sells all things Moroccan, from rugs, ornate jewellery boxes, lamps and cushions to scarves and pointy-toed slippers. Good gift-hunting territory.
☎ 324 3436 ✉ Palmotićeva 19 🕙 10am-6pm 🚊 Trg Republike

ARTS, CRAFTS & GIFTS

For some real Serbian antiquities and oddities you could do worse than explore the Kalenić Pijaca market on a Saturday morning (see box p28). The market stalls around Kalemgdan Citadel sometimes sell communist-era badges, buttons and other kitsch knick-knacks.

Beogradski Izlog (3, C3)
A centrally located shop selling a range of surprisingly nontacky Belgrade-themed souvenirs plus some stylish stationery, ceramics, T-shirts, posters and postcards.
☎ 631 721 ✉ Kneza Mihailova 6 🕙 9am-8pm Mon-Sat, 10am-8pm Sun 🚊 Trg Republike

Ethnographic Museum Shop (3, C2)
The Ethnographic Museum's small but well-stocked shop sells brightly coloured, hand-crafted ethnic fabrics, pots and knick-knacks.
☎ 328 1888 ✉ Studentski Trg 13 🕙 10am-5pm Tue-Sat, 9am-2pm Sun 🚊 Studentski Trg

BOOKS & MUSIC

Mamut (3, C3)
Three floors of books, magazines and newspapers in English as well as CDs, DVDs and gifts. Mamut is also strong on dance music, alternative rock and modern Serbian music.
☎ 639 060 ✉ cnr Kneza Mihailova & Sremska 🕙 9am-10pm Mon-Sat, noon-10pm Sun 🚊 Trg Republike

Plato Bookshop (3, B2)
One of two branches of Plato in Belgrade. This one has a larger range than the university store on Vase Carapića (although it has no Internet access or café). Stocks English literature, maps, books on Serbia and stationery.
☎ 625 834 ✉ 48 Knez Mihailova 🕙 9am-midnight Mon-Sat, noon-midnight Sun

Eating

You can eat and drink very well for very little money in Belgrade whether you browse on that ubiquitous Western Balkan street snack the *burek* (a filo-pastry pie filled with cheese, mince or potato) or tackle the usually heavier restaurant fare of grilled meats, moussaka, schnitzels and hearty stews.

Good seafood is rarer in the city but can be found if you know where to look. Portions range from large to impossible, so exercise restraint when ordering. Fresh vegetables and salads are easy to find and are dishes the Serbs do simply but well.

Perhaps the only criticism visitors will have, if they stay for more than a few days, is that alternatives to all that hearty, heavy food are not that profuse. Roasted and grilled meats really do predominate and international cuisine most often means pizza or pasta. Perhaps surprisingly (given Serbia's location and history), fresh, simple Turkish meze-style fare is hard to find and Belgrade has yet to blaze any kind of trail in modern gastronomy.

THE BILL

The price symbols in this chapter indicate the cost of a two-course meal for one, excluding drinks. There's generally no cover charge and, while tipping is always welcome, rounding up the bill to a convenient sum is acceptable in all but the finest restaurants, where the addition of around 10% is customary.

€	up to 300DIN
€€	300–800DIN
€€€	800–1400DIN
€€€€	over 1400DIN

BELGRADE'S TOP FIVE

Zaplet (p35) – Light, modern, tasty Serbian food served in smart surroundings in Belgrade's inner suburbs.

Guštimora (p35) – Earn your lunch exploring nearby Ada Ciganlija (p15) then devour Guštimora's fresh, simple seafood just across the water.

? (p31) – Delightfully atmospheric interior, excellent Serbian food, traditional music, mustachioed waiters and unquestionably great value.

Kalemegdanska Terasa (p31) – Magnificent, romantic terrace views, good Serbian and Italian food.

Byblos (p34) – Fresh, simple, clean Lebanese flavours with lots of veggie options.

KALEMEGDAN & OLD TOWN

? (3, B3)
Traditional Serbian €€
The name may be puzzling but there's no question about this being one of the best places in town for traditional Serbian food, décor and atmosphere. Inside the rustic, lopsided, 19th-century timber exterior you'll find a cramped but cosy Serbian tavern with low tables, traditional music and excellent, inexpensive Serbian dishes such as slow-cooked sausage and beans (like Gascon cassoulet) and tender lamb or veal *ispod saca* (baked under hot coals in a special earthenware pot).
☎ 635 421 ✉ Kralja Petra 6 🕑 7am-11pm (no food served Sun nights) 🚋 2, 11, 13

Greenet (3, C3)
Café €€
The cosy Greenet chain is becoming the Starbucks of Belgrade, with several branches around the city serving good lattes and cappuccinos, and a range of cakes. Unusually for Belgrade, there's the option to buy them to take away.
☎ 323 8474 ✉ Nušićeva 8 🕑 8am-8pm 🚋 Trg Republike

Hot Spot Café (3, C2)
Café & Bar €
A contemporary, glass-fronted bar-cum-café overlooking a leafy square. Good for breakfast/brunch including freshly squeezed orange juice, toasted sandwiches and delicious coffee. Cranks up a bit in the evenings with house and dance beats.
☎ 263 905 ✉ Studentski Trg 2 🕑 8am-12am daily 🚋 Studentski Trg

Jevrem (3, C2)
Traditional Serbian €€
In a lovingly restored old Dorćol house with a cool garden terrace, this is an elegant place to browse on simple but well executed Serbian classics. We recommend the Serbian beans, accompanied by one of the wines from the excellent selection.
☎ 328 4746 ✉ Gospodar Jevremova 36 🕑 10am-2am Mon-Sat, 2-10pm Sun 🚋 Trg Republike 🅿

Kalemegdanska Terasa (1, B1)
Serbian €€€
Occupying a prime viewpoint high in the grounds of Kalemegdan Citadel, this wins Belgrade's dining-with-a-view prize by a mile (if the weather permits terrace dining, that is). The peach-walled, faux-ancient interior is less exciting. The creditable food – grilled meat, cutlets and some Italian fare – is tasty, but perhaps a little too staid and traditional to truly live up to the knockout location.
☎ 328 2727 ✉ Kalemegdan bb 🕑 noon-1am 🚋 Beko

Kapric (3, C2)
Italian €€€
Laid-back and intimate, Kapric offers a slightly better class of pizza and pasta than the nearby Kosova, with a few local appetisers thrown in, such as Serbian prosciutto. The portions are huge.
☎ 262 5930 ✉ Kralja Petra 44 🕑 lunch & dinner Mon-Sat 🚋 Studentski Trg

Loki (3, C1)
Fast food €
It's late, you're having trouble focusing on this page and your beer-bloated belly is demanding some ballast. The solution? Join the line outside the green shed known as Loki and order its excellent *spljeskavica* (a Serbian burger).
✉ Kralja Petra 🕑 24hr 🚋 Studentski Trg 🅿 🔥 fair

Freshly baked goodies at Pekara Centar Pizza (p32)

Opera (3, C3)
Italian €€€
Appealing for many reasons including the central location, tables lit by smart green overhead lamps and the summer terrace looking onto the pedestrianised part of Obilićev venac combined with a simple, mainly Italian menu. The best options are the appetisers and light lunch dishes (including beef *carpaccio, bruschetta*, zucchini stuffed with ham, sour cream, parmesan and mozzarella) rather than the more pedestrian main courses. Also good just for a coffee and something sweet.
☎ 303 6200 ✉ Obilićev venac 30 🕑 10am-midnight 🚊 Trg Republike ♿ fair

Pekara Centar Pizza
(3, C3)
Snacks & Pizza €
One of the most convenient places for a pit stop day or night, this central 24-hour bakery serves freshly baked pizzas and pastries plus

Warm glow from a café on Kneza Mihailova

French bread and pretzels.
✉ Kolarčeva 10 🕑 24hr 🚊 Trg Republike ♿ good

Peking Restaurant
(3, C2)
Chinese €€€
The striking red lanterns and Chinese décor look authentic and although none of the staff is Chinese, the food tastes like pretty much any other equivalent Chinese in the world, with only a few Serb-influenced curveballs, such as duck with walnuts or deep-fried ice cream.
☎ 181 931 ✉ Vuka Karadžića 2 🕑 11am-midnight Mon-Sat, 2pm-midnight Sun 🚊 Trg Republike

Plato (3, C2)
Italian €€
Plato (plar-to) is an eclectic mix of restaurant, café, bar and live-music venue. It provides light lunch-style food, mostly Italian and a relaxed atmosphere in which to eat, drink and listen to what's playing (usually jazz or Cuban rhythms).
☎ 658 863 ✉ Akademski Plato 1 🕑 9am-2am Mon-Thu, 9am-3am Fri, 10am-3am Sat, noon-2am Sun 🚊 Studentski Trg

¿Que Pasa? (3, B2)
International €€€
Is it a busy restaurant with a great bar, or a funky bar that does food? The menu is a curious mishmash of Mexican and Serbian, and the music is definitely Latin. A stylish place where business folk unwind, although the mindless Fashion TV endlessly showing on the plasma screens is annoying.

☎ 330 5377 🖳 www.que-pasa.co.yu ✉ Kralja Petra 13-15 🕑 8am-midnight 🚊 2, 11, 13 Ⓥ

Russian Tsar (3, C3)
A Belgrade institution, this grandiose, old-world café was closed for an extensive refurbishment at the time of writing. With luck it should reopen better than before but hopefully with the heavy chandeliers back in place and with the atmosphere of a Moscow salon still intact. Good for breakfast, teas, coffees and alcoholic drinks, plus there's a leafy garden for summer.
☎ 633 628 ✉ Obilićev venac 28 🕑 8am-midnight 🚊 Trg Republike

Trattoria Košava (3, B2)
Italian & Balkan €€
An intimate little place serving decent, if not award-winning, pasta, pizza and mushroom risotto plus a few specialities including local hare and (gulp) 'young horse'.
☎ 627 344 ✉ Kralja Petra 36 🕑 9am-1am Mon-Fri, noon-1am Sat & Sun 🚊 Studentski Trg

Tribeca (3, B2)
International €€€
Too cool for school restaurant/lounge Tribeca is a stylish sort of place with plush furnishings, a well-heeled crowd and its own chill-out CD. The food is competent, vaguely international fare – such as chicken wrapped in prosciutto and filled mozzarella and sweet peppers – and the cocktails pack a punch.
☎ 328 5656 ✉ Kralja Petra 20 🕑 9-2am 🚊 Studentski Trg

SKADARSKA & AROUND

Cobbled, traffic-free and tree-shaded Skardaska is a pleasantly noise- and fume-free street lined with about a dozen restaurants and it's just a *burek*'s throw from the centre. If you just can't make your mind up, stroll down here, although it must be said that the predominance of traditional Serbian eateries means there's not a great deal of culinary variation.

Haunting Romany music accompanies the food at Šešir Moj

Guli (3, D2)
Italian €€

Modern, cosy, vaguely glam (local celebs meet and eat here), this is the place, on otherwise traditional Serbian Skadarska, for decent pasta and good, thin-crust pizza baked in a wood-fired oven. Good cocktails and an interesting selection of wines from Italy, Australia, Chile and Argentina.

☎ 323 7204 ✉ Skadarska 13 🕑 11am-1am 🚊 Trg Republike

Ikki (3, C2)
Japanese €€€

A welcome variation to meat-heavy Serbian nosh, but with typically sizeable Serbian-style portions (how very un-Japanese). The tempura and teriyaki are better than the sushi here, which doesn't quite have the requisite zing of absolute freshness. Takeaways also available.

☎ 2184 183 ✉ Gospodar Jovanova 46 🕑 noon-midnight 🚊 Trg Republike 🅿

Šešir Moj (3, D2)
Serbian €€

The flower-bedecked trellis and trickling water feature outside and a cosy interior give this place a rustic

...AND TO DRINK?

Don't dine without trying out some of the local hooch to accompany it. *Pivo* (beer) is universally available, but it's well worth seeking out Nikšićko *pivo* (both light and dark), brewed at Nikšić, in Montenegro. The darker version is a full-flavoured stout-style beer redolent of Guinness and molasses.

Many people distil their own *rakija* (brandy), made of grapes or out of plums (*šljivovica*). Other varieties include *orahovača* (walnut), *kruškovača* or *viljamovka* (pear) or *jabukovača* (apple). Ask for *domaca rakija* in a restaurant and you will be offered homemade *rakija* made of a choice of fruit.

Montenegrin red wine is usually rich and complex. Vranac, the most popular wine, is widely available.

A bittersweet aperitif, *pelinkovac*, a herbal, medicinal tasting liquor, is currently popular in Belgrade.

Coffee is traditionally served Turkish style, 'black as hell, strong as death and sweet as love', but superb espresso and cappuccino are easy to find. If you want anything other than herbal teas (camomile or hibiscus) ask for Indian tea.

romance only added to when a Roma band swirl in playing their hauntingly passionate music. The food is solid too. Try freshly baked corn bread, simple, flavour-packed salads or specialities such as *punjena bela vešalica* (pork fillet stuffed with *kajmak* – a salty cream cheese). Reasonable vegetarian options too. The pick of the Skadarska restaurants.
☎ 322 8750 ✉ Skadarska 21 ☼ 8am-late 🚌 Trg Republike Ⓥ

Srpska Kafana (3, E3)
Serbian €€
Occupying the outer reaches of the city centre, this place serves traditional Serbian food every bit as good as those on Skadarska, but for significantly less money. It specialises in hearty, earthy dishes such as breaded veal tripe, homemade sausages and barbecue platters.
☎ 324 7197
✉ Svetogorska 25
☼ 9am-midnight 🚌 28, 41

The Belgrade smart set head for the pizzas at Guli (p33)

Writers' Club (Klub Književnika) (3, D3)
Serbian €€
Popular since the Tito era, when it was the haunt of the state-approved literati, this grand old mansion restaurant and its white-jacketed waiters remain a traditional Belgrade favourite. The club may not have the cachet it once did but at least the stuffed zucchini and roast lamb with potatoes have kept their cult status.
✉ Francuska 7 ☼ 6pm-1am 🚌 Trg Republike

TAŠMAJDAN & SLAVIJA

Byblos (3, E6)
Lebanese €€€
Revive tastebuds jaded by all that heavy meat with the 40 fresh, light meze choices at this intimate, softly lit basement place with a vaulted brick ceiling. Grilled haloumi, mini-chicken pies, falafel or broad bean dip in tahini are typical and excellent. The mains, with three vegetarian options including vegetarian moussaka, are fine but stick to the meze list unless you're ravenous.
☎ 244 1938 ✉ Kneginje Zorke 30 ☼ noon-1 am 🚌 Slavija Ⓟ Ⓥ

Dom lovaka (3, E6)
Serbian €€
Tucked away a short stroll from the Park Hotel and the many bars along Njegoševa. The wall-mounted deer antlers and black timber beams lend it a hunting lodge air, appropriately enough since game is Dom

lovaka's speciality. Wild boar sausages, tender fillets of doe, deer stew with dumplings all feature, washed down with a good Vranac or the agreeable Nikšićko dark beer.
☎ 436 128
✉ Alekse Nendoovica 19 ☼ 10am-11.30pm
🚌 Slavija

Madera (3, E5)
Serbian €€€
The art deco aesthetic, dark wood floors, high ceilings and fantastic dining terrace facing Tašmadjan Park set the tone. Crisp white linen, freshly baked rolls and a good wine list confirm first impressions and the kitchen turns out exemplary grilled meat and roast lamb full of flavour. If only the chef had a little more appetite for culinary experimentation.
☎ 323 1332
🖥 www.maderarestoran.com
✉ Bulevar Kralija Aleksandra 43
☼ 10am-1am 🚌 27
♿ fair

NEW BELGRADE & ZEMUN

Aleksandar (2, off A1)
Fish €€
Right on the banks of the Danube, this place offers an extensive fish menu drawn from both sea and river. Try the fiery-red *riblja čorba* (a peppery fish soup), served with a huge hunk of bread to mop up the remains.
☎ 199 462 ✉ Kej Oslobođenja 49, Zemun
☼ 9am-midnight
🚌 84 Ⓟ

Focaccia (2, B3)
Italian & Mediterranean €€€
Very high-end food and prices, as you might expect for the Hyatt Regency's flagship restaurant, Focaccia is an impeccably elegant place, with zesty, clean Italian and southern French flavours and a great wine list to match. Dinner only (except for the excellent weekend brunch).
☎ 301 1143 ✉ Hyatt Regency, New Belgrade ☽ 7-11pm 🚌 73, 83 Ⓟ

Danubius (2, off A1)
Fish & Meat €€
One of several waterside restaurants in sleepy, charming Zemun, Danubius specialises in river fish, including catfish and pike perch but if you don't fancy those, there's always the inevitable meat dishes.
☎ 617 233 ✉ Kej Oslobođenja 57, Zemun ☽ 10-1am 🚌 84 Ⓟ

WORTH A TRIP

Dačo (2, off F2)
Traditional Serbian €€
A local legend, the all-Serbian Dačo is worth the taxi ride for the waiters in national dress, the traditional musicians and the boisterous sing-along from fellow diners (you have been warned). The entrées – *kajmak*, cheeses, *pršuta* (prosciutto) and other cold meats and salad items – served on wooden platters are the restaurant's speciality. Book ahead.
☎ 278 1009 ✉ Patrisa Lumumbe 49 ☽ 10.30am-midnight Ⓟ

SERBIAN FOOD. FAST.
For those able to walk and chew at the same time, there are bakeries and fast food kiosks dotted all over town and offering an inexpensive but delicious taste of savoury and sweet Serbian and Turkish classics to go. Look out for *bureks*, *gibanica* (cheese pies), *spljeskavica* (a Serbian burger) and *yiros* (meat in pitta bread), as well as sweet pastries including Baklava and strudels.

Good examples include **Loki** (p31) and **Pekara Aça** (3, E3; ☎ 3234 673; Svetogorska 25; ☽ 8am-7pm; 🚌 28, 41). More of a high-end patisserie than anything else and one of the finest bakeries in town, it serves some exquisite sweet and savoury morsels, including bite-size choux pastries with ham and cheese, and rich, heavenly, chocolate-coated chestnuts.

Guštimora (2, off A5)
Fish €€€
A relative newcomer, Guštimora serves the best seafood we've tasted in Belgrade, based on simple Mediterranean recipes that don't mess with the freshness of the raw materials. There's good fish soup, pasta and risotto, including a black squid ink risotto.
☎ 3551 268 ✉ Radniča 27 ☽ noon-midnight 🚌 87 bus terminus Ⓟ

Priroda (2, off F4)
Vegetarian & Vegan €
It may be a long taxi ride east of the centre but vegetarians and vegans will gratefully make the pilgrimage to this excellent meat-free haven in the City of Carnivores, with a menu of delicately flavoured vegetables and pulses.
☎ 411 890 ✉ Batutova 11 ☽ 12.30-9.30pm Ⓟ ♿ fair ♿ Ⓥ

Zaplet (2, F4)
Modern Serbian €€€
Zaplet's light, fresh, contemporary take on Serbian and Mediterranean dishes means food that's full of flavour and freshness and some way ahead of the next best in town. There are some excellent vegetarian options like mushrooms on sage polenta or ratatouille and mozzarella tart. Stylish surroundings, middling desserts. Worth the taxi ride.
☎ 240 4142 ✉ cnr Kajmakcalanska & Zarka Zrenjanina ☽ 9am-midnight Tue-Sun 🚌 25, 26 Ⓟ Ⓥ

Entertainment

Belgrade's single biggest attraction must be its bar and clubbing scene, which is vibrant, eclectic, cutting-edge and terrific value. It doesn't matter what night it is, there's always a party going on somewhere. Drinks are cheap and entry to the many club nights is free. In summer things really get cranked up a notch aboard the dozens of riverside barges that serve as giant floating nightclubs (see p39).

Belgraders love their music; you can hear pretty much every genre and subgenre of modern popular music as well as classical (Belgrade has its own orchestra) and more typically Balkan sounds such as haunting Romany music and turbo folk, Serbia's saccharine, Euro-pop-style dance music. The performing arts are somewhat less well patronised and most productions are in Serbian.

The ticketing agency **Bilet Servis** (3, C3; ☎ 628 342; Trg Republike 5; ☽ 9am-8pm Mon-Fri, 9am-3pm Sat) sells tickets for many concert and theatre performances.

Seek out the stylish Ben Akiba bar

BARS

Ben Akiba (3, D3)
It's worth making the effort to find this convivial but elusive place, hidden up a flight of stairs inside an obscure courtyard and locked behind a thick door. Originally a haven for thirsty liberals fighting against the Milošević regime, it's now a popular watering hole for a stylish 30-something crowd.
☎ 323 7775 ✉ Nušićeva 8 ☽ 9am-late daily ᨎ Trg Republike

Federal Association of World Travellers (3, D3)
A welcoming, atmospheric place hidden behind a big black gate, and crammed with bohemian *objets d'art* and lush, theatrical furnishings. Very popular with foreign diplomats, aid workers and several resident cats. It's usually a relaxed place to sit and talk, although the occasional house parties are wild, loud and fun.
☎ 324 2303 ✉ 29 Novembra 7 ☽ 1pm-midnight Mon-Fri, 3pm-late Sat & Sun ᨎ Trg Republike

Gaudi (3, C2)
A stylish little bar away from the showboating just over the way in Strahinjića Bana street. The crowd is well heeled, the music is mellow, and there's a garden terrace.
☎ 182 849 ✉ Gospodar Jevremova 40 ☽ 10am-2am daily ᨎ Studentski Trg

Idiot (3, E3)
Art students, musicians and a mixed straight and gay crowd of both sexes make this cosy little basement bar, with an appealing summer terrace, a model of inclusion and laid-back cool. The music is leftfield rock and electronica, but not so loud you can't chat.
✉ Dalmastinska 13 ☽ Noon-2am daily ᨎ trolleybus 28

Jazz Café (3, C3)
You won't necessarily hear jazz here, either live or piped, but it's one of several cosy little bars along this end of Oblićev venac, most of them with a pub-like lack of pretension and inexpensive drinks.
☎ 328 2380 ✉ Oblićev venac ⊙ 10am-2am 🚊 Trg Republike

Kandahar (3, D2)
One of the more relaxed places that line the fabled Silicon Valley (see box), this intimate basement bar decked out in faux-Arabic décor and low-level seating on benches and scatter cushions offers good cocktails, exotic teas and coffee with Turkish delight.
☎ 064 334 3970 ✉ Strahinjića Bana 48 ⊙ 8am-late 🚊 Studentski Trg

Monin Bar (3, D2)
Monin's chic, spacious, cleverly lit interior – all plate glass and vaulted ceilings covered in billowy white fabric – makes it perhaps the most appealing of Belgrade's 'style' bars. The waiters are attentive, the music is loungey and the bar staff mix a mean Negroni.
☎ 065 3 999 998 ✉ Dositejeva 9a ⊙ 11am-1am 🚊 Trg Republike

Movie Bar (3, C3)
A stylish, central place ideally located to kick the evening off with an inexpensive cocktail while listening to down-tempo pop and jazz. Serves Italian-style aperitivo snacks and wine between 5pm and 8pm.

☎ 262 3818 ✉ Kolarčeva 6 ⊙ 9am-1am 🚊 Trg Republike

Pazi Škola! (3, E3)
A great bar inside the same nightclub building as Plastic (see p38), Pazi Škola! is a blue room with a few sofas, tables and chairs, as well as a bit of standing room, so everyone can fit in. Best classed as a DJ bar, it's subdued on weeknights, with a few barflies enjoying a quiet drink, and kicking at weekends, with most of Belgrade's 'alternative' club crowd dancing until all hours.
☎ 328 5437 ✉ cnr Dalmatinska & Takovska ⊙ 7pm-1am Mon-Thu, 7pm-late Fri, Sat & Sun 🚊 trolleybus 28

Rezime (3, B2)
A classy, calm and civilised little café/bar with green leather armchairs inside an ornate art nouveau building, it's a popular meeting place for businessmen and ladies who lunch. Good hot chocolate. A pianist tickles the ivories at weekends.

☎ 328 4276 ✉ Kralja Petra 41 ⊙ 8am-midnight

Sports Café (3, C3)
Smart, modern but pretty soulless, Sport Café is only really a place to come if you want live football, including the European and English premierships, and pretty much any big sporting event.
☎ 3243 177 ✉ Makedonska 4 ⊙ 9am-1am Mon-Sat, 11am-1am Sun 🚊 Trg Republike

CLUBS

Akademija (3, B2)
The seminal '80s Belgrade club, this dingy, graffiti-plastered place is coming back into vogue with a younger, studenty crowd, after a lull in the '90s. The ragged, dark interior won't win any awards but it's about the music here. There's everything from rap and reggae to drum 'n' bass and live bands such as local heroes Darkwood Dub.
☎ 627 846 🖳 www.akademija.net ✉ Rajićeva 10 ⊙ 10pm-late Tue-Sun 🚇 Kalmegdan

---

SILICON VALLEY
By day Strahinjića Bana, in a leafy part of Dorćol, is a quiet street lined with a string of fashionable bars. But as the witching hour approaches, you'll understand why the locals call it 'Silicon Valley': well-endowed trophy girlfriends arrive with their gangsta boyfriends and the bars quickly fill to bursting. As well as its share of menacing-looking heavies and their manicured molls, this street is also popular with local celebrities, earning it the alternative nickname of 'Ostrich Street' (because every time anyone enters a bar everyone else cranes their necks to see if they are a local celeb).

Andergraund (3, B2)
Belgraders party hard inside this cavernous and justly revered nightspot. On Fridays there's hip hop with an R&B tinge but the place really catches fire on Saturdays when big-name European DJs play house-style beats to packed crowds.
☎ 625 681 ⌨ www .andergraund.com ✉ Pariška 1a ⏱ noon-midnight Sun-Thu, to 2am Fri & Sat 🚋 Kalmegdan ♿ excellent

Bar Balthazar (3, A2)
It's hard to define the exact appeal of this jumping little place, downstairs in a brick basement a hop and a skip from Andergraund. Perhaps it's the music policy of dancey, accessible house with some guitar stuff thrown in or the fact that every subset of Belgrade's youth crams in here, be they ravers, fashionistas, rappers or rockers. Lots of fun and very friendly.
☎ 706 3302 ✉ Karadjordjeva 9 € free ⏱ 10pm-late 🚋 2, 11, 13

Live music, cultural events, Internet café, bar...it's all happening at Dom Omladine (p40)

Ellington's (2, B3)
A plush bar-cum-nightclub inside the Hyatt Regency (p43) with a generally older, business clientele, good cocktails and a cigar bar. Lacks atmosphere a tad in the absence of a live band but does host lively sessions at weekends.
☎ 311 1234 ✉ Milentija Popovica, Hyatt Regency

Hotel ⏱ 9.30pm-2.30am 🚋 11 ♿ good

Oh! Cinema! (1, C2)
A rock-till-dawn café/bar on the eastern bulwarks of the citadel, occupying a great spot overlooking the Danube and zoo. Occasional live music.
☎ 328 4000 ✉ Kalemegdan Citadel ⏱ 9pm-5am (summer only) 🚋 Kalemegdan

Plastic (3, E3)
More intimate than Andergraund (see above), Plastic has great DJs playing electronica that ranges from house to trance and techno. The fired-up but friendly alternative crowd creates an electric atmosphere on the dance floor but there's also space to chill out in the bar, Pazi Škola. (p37).
✉ cnr Dalmatinska & Takovska ⏱ 11pm-late Fri & Sat only 🚌 trolleybus 28

GAY BELGRADE
Gay people don't generally feel hugely well tolerated in Serbia, which may be part of the reason why there's not a large or especially confident gay scene, nor a terribly visible gay community.

One dedicated gay club for men (and a few straight women) is **Club X** (3, D3; cnr Makedonska & Svetogorska; 10pm-late Fri & Sat; € 200DIN). It's a scruffy, dingy basement bar that appears rather cruisey on first acquaintance and plays a pretty woeful blend of Euro pop and bad disco. In fact, if you can stand the music, it turns out to be a very relaxed and friendly place. The excellent **Idiot** (p36) is one of the few watering holes that have an overt gay and lesbian clientele.

Šargon (3, A2)

Next door to Andergraund (see left) but with a markedly different atmosphere. It's all disco, disco, disco here, with '80s and '90s music and a more subdued crowd. Nevertheless, it's packed at weekends.

☎ 063 667 722 ✉ Pariška 1a 🕙 noon-midnight Sun-Thu, noon-2am Fri & Sat 🚋 Kalemegdan

Stefan Braun (3, C5)

Pass the black Humvee and the bull-necked bouncers, ride the elevator up this ugly tower block and prepare for whooping, whistling, dancing and mayhem when the door opens. Terrific, hard-edged house and an up-for-it (chemically assisted?) crowd give this place a charged atmosphere. Imagine a rave in a speakeasy. In summer the club moves venue, so phone ahead.

☎ 065 5566 456 ✉ Nemanjina 4 🕙 10pm-5am 🚋 trolleybus 41

DANUBE RIVER BARGES

One of the great attractions of Belgrade in summer is the dozens of barges lining the Danube and Sava Rivers, which serve as floating nightclubs. The most concentrated grouping lies along a kilometre of the Danube adjacent to the Hotel Jugoslavia in Novi Beograd. Many barges are closed in winter.

A strip of floating bars, restaurants and discos also lines the west bank of the Sava River. Get there by walking over Brankov Most or by taking tram 7, 9 or 11. Most of these are only open in summer.

Acapulco (2, off A1)

Crop-haired muscle men come here to flaunt their money, their chunky jewellery and especially their colt-legged 'sponsorship girls' (who accompany them in return for gifts rather than out of love). The music is fast and furious turbofolk and the atmosphere can be a tad edgy.

☎ 784 760 ✉ Bulevar Nikole Tesle 🕙 noon-3am 🚋 15, 704, 706, 707

Amfora (2, off A1)

A relaxed and stylish alternative to all the other big boat parties, this has the atmosphere of a plush hotel bar by the river, with comfy seating and low-level music. There's a smart dress code.

☎ 699 789 ✉ Bulevar Nikole Tesle 🕙 10pm-1am 🚋 15, 704, 706, 707

Bibis (2, off A1)

A subdued place, good for a chat and a drink before hitting its larger and louder neighbouring barges for an all-nighter. Popular in winter when other barges close.

☎ 319 2150 ✉ Bulevar Nikole Tesle 🕙 10pm-2am 🚋 15, 704, 706, 707

Exil (2, B2)

Relentlessly fast, pounding techno is the unwavering musical policy at this high-energy party barge on the western bank of the Sava.

✉ Savski Kej 🕙 noon-3am 🚋 7, 9,11

Monza (2, off A1)

Less of a nightclub, more of an afternoon place where you can sunbathe on the large outdoor terrace and listen to R&B.

☎ 319 0712 ✉ Bulevar Nikole Tesle 🕙 10am-1am 🚋 15, 704, 706, 707

LIVE MUSIC

Black Panther (2, A5)

It takes a huge effort to get to this small, remote barge and you take pot luck in winter, when there may be no other visitors. But in summer it comes alive with visitors attracted to the excellent Romany music. Note that this is a taxi ride away from the city centre.

✉ Savski Kej, Ada Ciganlija 🕙 8pm-late

All aboard the Monza for dancing and drinking into the small hours

Catch a Serbian cinema classic – or just enjoy the popcorn

Dom Omladine (3, D3)
This youth cultural centre has a full and frequent programme of jazz and pop music concerts as well as film festivals and multimedia events. There's also a relaxing café in the foyer.
☎ 324 8202
✉ Makedonska 22
☽ daily ▣ Trg Republike

Kolarčev University Concert Hall (3, C2)
The Belgrade Philharmonic Orchestra often performs at this elegant old concert hall just opposite the park and the trolleybus station.
☎ 630 550 ✉ Studentski Trg 5 ☽ box office 10am-noon & 6-8pm
▣ Studentski Trg

Sava Centar (2, A3)
A cavernous conference and concert venue across the river in Novi Beograd

that plays host to the few large international acts that do make it to town, as well as orchestras, the odd jazz band and numerous popular Balkan crooners and musicians.
☎ 213 9840 ▣ www.savacentar.com ✉ Milentija Popovića 9, Novi Beograd
⒭ Novi Beograd ♿ fair

Serbian Academy of Arts & Sciences (3, B2)
A small, intimate venue that plays host to a number of free concerts and exhibitions. There's no box office so check the window for details.
☎ 334 2400 ✉ Knez Mihailova 35 ☽ concerts 6pm Mon & Thu ▣ Trg Republike

SKC (Student Cultural Center) (3, D5)
Regularly hosts live music as well as some massive club nights with big-name

European DJs, such as Deep Dish, plus major bands from the Balkans, Western Europe and North America. It also stages art exhibitions and films.
☎ 360 2000 ▣ www.skc.org.yu ✉ cnr Kralja Milana & Resavska ☽ 8pm-late
▣ 19, 21, 22, 29

Tramvaj (3, F5)
A scruffy British pub-style place with live music every night and free passive smoking for every customer. Competent (if not always earth-shatteringly good) folk, rock and especially jazz musicians play here.
☎ 340 8269
✉ Ruzveltova 2 ☽ 8pm-4am ▣ trolleybus 28

CINEMA

Tuckwood Cineplex (3, D4)
A modern cineplex that offers the best surroundings in which to watch a film, although the programme tends to be along Hollywood blockbuster, rather than art house, lines. Films are either in English or with English subtitles.
☎ 323 6517 ✉ Kneza Miloša 7
▣ 40, 41

Yugoslav Film Library Theatre (3, D3)
This museum is not only the home of the bulk of Yugoslav film archives, it also screens classic Balkan and European classic cinema. See its monthly programme for more details.
☎ 324 8250 ▣ www.kinoteka.org.yu ✉ Kosovska 11 ☽ 11am-7pm Tue-Sun
▣ Trg Republike

SPORT

Football

Serbs have passionate, often quite violent allegiances to their local football clubs, to the extent that vanloads of fully tooled-up riot police attend even minor fixtures to keep the peace. Serbs also avidly follow English and European premierships and proudly point to several Serb players in these competitions. The country has recently put itself on the map by qualifying for the 2006 World Cup (and defeating Croatia's team on the same night).

The two big clubs in town are **FC Crvena Zvezda** (Red Star; 2, D6; ☎ 662 341; Ljutice Bogdana 1; 🚌 42, 58, 78) and **FC Partizan** (2, D5; ☎ 648 222; Humska 1; 🚌 trolley-bus 41). Derbies between these two teams are lively, sometimes incendiary, affairs. Tickets for big local and international fixtures sell out early so book well ahead.

Basketball

Serbs are almost as mad about basketball as they are about football and with good reason; their national basketball team, one of the best in the world, has won three European championships and won the world championship in 2003. The home grounds of Belgrade's teams, Crvena Zvzda (Red Star) and Partizan (both confusingly named after their footballing equivalents), are inside **Kalemegdan Citadel** (p8).

SPECIAL EVENTS

February to March *FEST film festival* (www.fest.org.yu) – International and local films are screened, with talks by various directors.

July *ECHO* – Belgrade's answer to the huge EXIT rock and pop festival in Novi Sad. Attracts increasingly big names, including Morcheeba.

August *Belgrade Beer Festival* (www.belgradebeerfest.com).

September *BITEF international theatre festival* (www.bitef.co.yu) – Originating in the avant-garde theatre of the '60s and '70s, it now showcases Serbia's best thespian talent and international theatre companies.

October *BEMUS music festival* (www.bemus.co.yu) – A classical music festival with a good choice of local and international artists.

Jazz festival – (usually late October).

Sleeping

If you've never stayed in Belgrade before, lower your expectations now. Apart from the deluxe places listed here, which wouldn't shame any major Western city, the bulk of Belgrade's hotels are stuck in a communist-era time warp.

While the city and the big hotel groups sort out the post-communist and post–civil war mess of property and development law, its hotel guests cry out for something better. In too many hotels fittings are old and often broken or missing (as, it seems, is the will to fix them). The lighting can be of the depressingly low-wattage and fluorescent variety, the hallways and lobbies tinged with an ever-present fug of cigarette smoke and the breakfasts are generally pretty meagre.

The good news is that many of the midrange places we've included below are starting to modernise, the high-end hotels are relatively good value by international standards and, even at the most visually neglected of the old hotels, service is usually warm while the most important basics (like crisp, clean bed linen and hot water) are a given.

ROOM RATES

These categories indicate the cost per night of a standard double room in high season.

Deluxe	from €250
Top End	€110–250
Midrange	€50–110
Budget	€20–50

LIVE LIKE A KING

Far and away the best hotel in town is the small all-suite hotel **Aleksander Palas** (3, B2; ☎ 330 5300 ▯ www.aleksandarpalas.com ✉ Kralja Petra 13-15 ▣ 2, 11, 13 Ⓟ garage ✕ cafés, bar & restaurant ▣ ▯), named after King Alexander (p46). It's ideally located, lavishly but stylishly furnished and hugely well appointed.

Inside the green-roofed, cream-yellow 19th-century building, each suite has a living room decked out with DVD players and multispeaker home cinema systems, a bedroom with a large, comfortable bed and a bathroom featuring a power shower so advanced it comes with its own instruction manual. There's wireless Internet throughout, a guests-only café terrace with river views, and good eating and drinking options in the attached restaurants and bar.

DELUXE

Hyatt Regency (2, B3)
Modern, stately and with the full complement of marble, mod cons, mutedly expensive décor and business-oriented services you would expect from the Hyatt chain, this is easily the next best hotel in town after the Aleksander Palas (see opposite). The downside, and it's a big one, is its location – stuck out in the middle of boring old Novi Beograd.
☎ 301 1234 ▣ www.belgrade.regency.hyatt.com ✉ Milentija Popovića 5 ▣ 11 P garage ♿ fair ✕ cafés, restaurants, bars ⚡ ▣ ◉

TOP END

Hotel Zlatnik (2, off A1)
One of the best Belgrade hotels for its high standards, warm service, and excellent facilities, it's unfortunately also one of the most remote. Located in a sleepy Zemun suburb, it's ideal if you want to stay outside the big smoke or if you need quick access to the airport. The cheerful, individually decorated rooms and fittings are to the highest standards and there's a good restaurant serving fish and Serbian classics.
☎ 316 7511 ▣ www.hotelzlatnik.com ✉ Slavonska 26, Zemun P off street ✕ restaurant

Le Petit Piaf (3, D2)
Right in the middle of Skardarska, the restaurant street, and close to antique shops and art galleries, Le Petit Piaf is a swish, contemporary-style small hotel with 12 rooms and mini apartments (all well equipped, with hairdryers, wireless Internet, air-con, etc) in a cute little mews with lots of natural light and an appealing summer terrace courtyard.
☎ 303 52 52 ▣ www.petitpiaf.com ✉ Skadarska 34 ▣ Trg Republike ✕ ⚡ ▣

Šumadija Hotel (2, off A5)
Very much a business hotel, handy for the Belgrade Fair conference centre and the leafy island of Ada Ciganlija (but little else), this Best Western franchise is modern, stylish and spotless with bright, cheerful rooms, a 24-hour business centre, a smart restaurant and a pleasing summer terrace.
☎ 305 4100 ▣ www.sumadija.com ✉ Šumadijski Trg 8 ▣ 11 ✕ restaurant & café ⚡ ▣

Ask for a room at the top for great views from the Hotel Balkan

MIDRANGE

Hotel Balkan (3, C3)
Less grandiose than the Moscow opposite but crucially ridding itself floor by floor of the usual dull rooms with a fresh, bright contemporary look and sparkly new fittings throughout. Rooms are spacious and the views down to Terazije street and across the city get better the higher you go.
☎ 268 7466 ▣ www.balkanhotel.net ✉ Prizrenska 2 ▣ Trg Republike ✕ café

Majestic (3, C3)
You can't get more central than the Majestic, just off the main square on a pedestrianised street near Obilicev venac's bar strip. The rooms in the new wing have been completely redone, with sparkling bathrooms, large TVs, cream walls, blue

throws and parquet floors. Alternatively go for the rather grand, ancient suites facing the street.

☎ 3285 777 🖳 www. majestic.co.yu ✉ Obilicev venac 28

🚋 Trg Republike

🅿 garage

Hotel Moscow (3, C4)

The most famous hotel in Belgrade and a lovely exterior it has too – a biscuit and jade-tiled art nouveau structure dating from 1906 with a large terrace out front. Rooms range from cheaper singles, which are small but comfortable (although the beds are tiny), to spacious doubles and luxurious apartments with writing desks that'll make you feel like Lord Byron. Try to get an exterior-facing, rather than a gloomy courtyard-facing room.

☎ 268 6255

🖳 hotelmoskva@absolutok. net ✉ Balkanska 🚋 Trg Republike 🍴

Hotel Palace (3, B3)

A notch up in standard from most state hotels (and slightly pricier as a result). The décor is positively modern 1990s, rather than the usual Cold War–era fittings, and most of the rooms are large, equipped with phones and TVs, and have spacious bathrooms. The service is generally eager and there's a good view of the city from the Panorama restaurant upstairs.

☎ 185 585 🖳 www. palacehotel.co.yu

✉ Topličin venac 23

🅿 garage

🍴 restaurant & café

BUDGET

Cheap hostel accommodation is scarce in Belgrade. Contact the Youth Hostel organisation (p54) for current hotel deals. It also books the **Jelica Milanović** (3, D5; ☎ 323 1268; Krunska 8; from €7.50 per person; ⏱ Jul & Aug), which offers its college dorms for use by visitors during the summer vacation.

Kasina Hotel (3, C3)

With the Balkan and the Moscow (see left), this is the third in the very central triangle of Belgrade hotels. The rooms are basic but decent and comfortable. Depending on whether you go for the 'comfort' or 'standard' option, you get air-conditioning and a minibar, or neither of those and slightly darker rooms. Try to nab one of the rooms overlooking the square.

☎ 323 5574 🖳 www. kasina.stari-grad.co.yu

✉ Terazije 25

🚋 Trg Republike

🍴 café

Hotel Royal (3, C2)

Possibly the best value for money in town: it's central (Dorćol area), cheap and clean. The rooms won't win any design awards but they are simply decorated and tidy (although new carpets wouldn't hurt) and the staff friendly. There is live music in the basement restaurant, if you're up for the folk experience.

☎ 634 222 🖳 www. hotelroyal.co.yu ✉ Kralja Petra 56 🚋 Studentski Trg

🍴 café & bar

Hotel Splendid (3, D4)

More splendid in name than in appearance, this place is frankly rather run down. Cigarette smoke from the public areas seems to creep into the rooms and the fittings are shabby. However, it's very cheap and very central (off Terazije) and the rooms facing the street have pleasing park views.

☎ 323 5444

🖳 www.splendid.co.yu

✉ Jovanovića 5

🚋 Trg Republike

🅿 public, opposite

🍴 café

Art nouveau splendour at the Hotel Moscow

About Belgrade

HISTORY
Early Inhabitants & the Arrival of Rome

Illyrians, Thracians and Celts all roamed across the Balkan Peninsula, including the area around Belgrade. But it was only when the Romans arrived and overthrew the Celts at Singidium (site of the present-day city) in the 3rd century BC that Belgrade's recorded history began.

In AD 395 Theodosius I divided the Roman Empire into two separate entities, the Western Roman Empire, centred on Rome, and the Eastern Roman Empire (later the Byzantine Empire), centred on Constantinople (now Istanbul). Serbia passed to the Byzantine Empire, leaving the future Belgrade, which abutted the border with the Western Roman Empire, at the leading edge of a religious, cultural, political and military fault line that would have heavy consequences for the city in the centuries to follow.

Slavic Rule, Christianity, Islam & Turkish Rule

During the 6th century, Slavic tribes crossed the Danube and occupied much of the Balkan Peninsula. In 879 Sts Cyril and Methodius converted the Serbs to Christianity. Serbian independence briefly flowered from 1217 with a 'Golden Age' during Stefan Dušan's reign (1346–55). After Stefan's death a long decline for Serbia, and thus also for Belgrade, set in.

At the pivotal Battle of Kosovo in 1389 the Turks defeated Serbia, ushering in 500 years of Islamic rule, mass migrations and the religious persecution and enslavement of non-Muslims. Belgrade itself, however, did not fall to the Turks until 1521, when it was besieged, overthrown and then burnt by Suleiman the Magnificent, sultan of the Ottoman Empire.

Bayrakli Mosque (p18): Belgrade's only surviving mosque

Independence

In the centuries following the Battle of Kosovo, there were many uprisings against Turkish rule but it was the widespread revolt of 1815 that led to de facto Serbian independence. This was brokered by the wily soldier and diplomat Miloš Obrenović, and it ultimately led to complete independence in 1878.

After this milestone Belgrade flourished. Many of its great buildings, including the Palace of Princess Ljubica, were constructed, and Belgrade also became something of a literary and educational centre.

A SICKLY ASSASSIN
If you had been strolling through Tašmajdan Park (p20) in 1912 you might have seen a sickly Bosnian Serb, Gavrilo Princip, being laughed at by his comrades on the park's firing range. The tubercular Princip was a terrible shot and by no means a natural soldier, nor for that matter, a natural terrorist. Undeterred by his feeble health, slight frame and lack of aim, however, he joined the secret Black Hand terrorist organisation, which was dedicated to the creation of a Greater Serbia and the defeat of the Austro-Hungarian Empire. By 1914 he had got his eye in, shooting Archduke Ferdinand dead in Sarajevo, an act that ultimately sparked two world wars.

The World Wars & the Birth of Yugoslavia

On 28 June 1914 Austria-Hungary used the assassination of Archduke Ferdinand by a Bosnian Serb as a pretext for invading Serbia, sparking WWI. After the war, Croatia, Slovenia, Bosnia and Hercegovina, Vojvodina, Serbia and its province Kosovo, as well as Montenegro and Macedonia joined to form the Kingdom of Serbs, Croats and Slovenes under King Alexander of Serbia. In 1929 the country was renamed Yugoslavia.

In March 1941 Yugoslavia joined the fascist Tripartite Alliance. This sparked a military coup and the country's abrupt withdrawal from the Alliance. Germany replied by bombing Belgrade.

The Communist Party, under Josip Broz Tito, assisted in the liberation of Yugoslavia. By 1945 the party had gained power; it abolished the monarchy, declared a federal republic and began hastily rebuilding Belgrade.

Cold War Yugoslavia

Tito broke with Stalin in 1948 and Yugoslavia became a nonaligned nation, belonging to neither of the two post-WWII power blocs led by the USA and the USSR respectively.

By 1986 Serbian nationalists were espousing the idea of a Greater Serbia, a doctrine adopted by Slobodan Milošević, the Serbian Communist Party leader. This horrified the other Soviet republics, which managed to gain independence by 1992.

While the violent collapse of Yugoslavia resulted in wars in neighbouring Croatia and in Bosnia and Hercegovina, the remaining parties of Serbia and Montenegro formed the 'third' Yugoslav federation in April 1992. The new constitution made no mention of 'autonomous provinces', infuriating Kosovar Albanians. Violence in Kosovo erupted in January 1998, provoked largely by the federal army and police, who moved to ethnically cleanse the country of its Albanian population. This galvanised NATO into a 78-day bombing campaign, with many of the bombs falling on Belgrade. On 12 June 1999 Serbian forces withdrew from Kosovo.

Belgrade Today

In the federal presidential elections of September 2000, the opposition, led by Vojislav Koštunica, declared victory. Milošević tried to cling on to power but mass demonstrations around the city and its parliament building, and the loss of key allies, ensured his defeat. In April 2001 he was arrested and extradited to stand trial at the International War Crimes Tribunal in The Hague.

After the dark Milošević years, life in Belgrade is slowly improving. The city is becoming reinvigorated, its clubs and pubs pulse with life and music and its economy growing, although many challenges remain and unemployment stays stubbornly high.

ENVIRONMENT

Air quality in Belgrade is a big problem, both indoors (because of smoking) and out on the streets (because of traffic fumes).

Some consequences of the NATO bombing campaign of 2000 are ecological hazards – such as the destruction of the bridges over the Danube which caused heavy river pollution – although none present direct danger to the visitor.

GOVERNMENT & POLITICS

Belgrade is the capital of a loose union of Serbia and Montenegro that was formed in April 2002 to replace an EU-brokered deal, and in 2006 a referendum was planned to test this settlement.

In March 2003 Zoran Đinđić, Serbia's first democratically elected prime minister since WWII, was assassinated in Belgrade (allegedly by crime bosses and former Milošević-era paramilitary commanders). Đinđić had been instrumental in handing over Milošević to the International War Crimes Tribunal and had been trying to purge politics and business of crime and corruption.

Inconclusive parliamentary elections in December 2003 resulted in a series of power-sharing deals which saw Vojislav Koštunica installed as head of a centre-right coalition. In June 2004, Serbia and Montenegro gained a new president in the pro-European Boris Tadić.

ECONOMY

The days of hyperinflation (see p48), sparked by the disastrous policies of the Milošević regime, are long gone and the country's economy is now largely stable, although Serbia's new government faces the huge task of rebuilding an economy shattered by sanctions, war and fiscal collapse.

It has already achieved a great deal, stabilising the dinar, reforming the banking sector and simplifying the taxation system.

Statuesque struggles outside the Parliament Building (p20)

Interest-free loans from the World Bank worth US$540 million and aid worth more than €200 million from the EU have helped, as has a steady increase in foreign investment. The drain of young talent from the country during the war years may be a more difficult and longer-term economic challenge.

SOCIETY & CULTURE

The cliché of the Serb national character is of a people with a warrior tradition – proud and generous, but violent when provoked and self-pitying when they've had a *šljivović* too many.

MONEY TO BURN

During the 1990s, economic sanctions and gross mishandling of the economy led to severe hyperinflation, the highest in European history. It became cheaper to use banknotes to paper walls than to buy wallpaper. At one point a 500 billion dinar banknote was issued, making every Serb an instant multibillionaire, but it had almost no buying power and destroyed at a stroke the bank savings of an entire nation. All over Belgrade, you can still purchase examples of these banknotes as souvenirs.

It's safe to say that the generous part is true. Serbs are incredibly friendly, open and gregarious almost without exception. The oppressive, xenophobic and paranoiac nationalism of the Milošević era set the clock back for many Belgraders, particularly the educated middle classes, who saw themselves as part of a progressive and cosmopolitan culture that was open to new ideas.

Many of them, the younger generation in particular, are busy rediscovering these ideals. They are forward looking, yearning for greater things, open to the idea of closer ties with the EU and seasoned connoisseurs of the music and cultural influences emanating from it.

That said, a darker culture of ultranationalism and resentful xenophobia, too often expressed in violence on the football terraces and fuelled perhaps by stubbornly high unemployment, maintains a hold. The nationalist far right remains a significant political force.

Religiously speaking, Belgrade, like Serbia as a whole, is Serb Orthodox although the city also has about 10,000 Muslims. There's also a small and visibly downtrodden Roma minority living in miserable shanty towns on the cultural, economic and geographical margins of the city.

ARTS
Literature

The oral tradition of epic poetry was first committed to paper by the 19th-century Belgrade writer and linguist Vuk Karadžić, who also reformed the language and formalised the rules of Serbian grammar. The epics were then translated into English, French and German by the likes of Goethe and Walter Scott.

Another significant figure in late-19th-century Serbian literature was Jovan Jovanović Zmaj (1833–1904), who wrote poetry, fiction and essays. Contemporary writers include the poet Vasko Popa, whose work has been translated into English and many other languages.

Other interesting reads are *In the Hold* by Vladimir Arsenijević, *Words Are Something Else* by David Albahari, *Petrija's Wreath* by Dragoslav Mihailović and *Fear and Its Servant* by Mirjana Novaković.

Bosnian-born but a past Belgrade resident, Ivo Andrić was awarded the Nobel Prize for Literature for his *Bridge over the Drina*. The excellent works of Danilo Kiš are available in English: *A Tomb for Boris Davidovich* is recommended.

The benchmark for travel writing on the region is *Black Lamb and Grey Falcon*, Rebecca West's account of her travels around the Balkans in the mid-

Belgrade's politicians and literati meet for dinner at the Writers' Club (p34)

20th century. Matthew Collins' *This Is Serbia Calling* (2004) is a compelling account of the struggle of a few idealists to resist and help overthrow the Milošević regime, a struggle depicted through the prism of the rock and dance music subcultures kept alive by Belgrade's iconic radio station B92.

Cinema & TV

Cinema is a thriving industry in Serbia, but not many of the films made in the country ever get past the borders of the former Yugoslavia, although it's possible to find some Serbian cinema classics with English subtitles in Serbia. Titles to look out for include *Ko to tamo peva?* (Who's That Singing Over There?), *Petrija's Wreath* and *Balkan Express*.

The award-winning film *Underground*, by Sarajevo-born director Emir Kusturica, is told in a chaotic, colourful style, reminiscent of Fellini's movies. Bosnian director Danis Tanović's *No Man's Land* superbly deals with an encounter between a Bosnian soldier and a Serb soldier stuck in a trench on their own during the Bosnian war.

> **DID YOU KNOW?**
> One of the main reasons for Belgrade's turbulent past is its status as a vital crossroads between East and West. The Morava valley route is virtually the only nonmountainous overland route from continental Europe to Greece and Asia Minor while the Danube River, which flows through Belgrade, links Western and Central Europe with the Black Sea to the East and, beyond that, Asia Minor and the Middle East.

Music

Serbia's vibrant traditional dances are led by musicians playing bagpipes, flutes and fiddles. *Blehmuzika* (brass music influenced by Turkish and Austrian military music) is the national music of Serbia, commonly played by Roma and often at weddings or funerals. One of the most popular recordings of this music is the soundtrack to the film *Underground* and albums by the trumpet player Boban Marković.

Modern music covers anything from wild Romany music to house, techno, blues, jazz and drum 'n' bass. Popular modern Serbian groups include Darkwood Dub and Eyesburn.

'Turbofolk', a more dubious Serb speciality, is the bastard child of the ethnic folk tradition and fast techno beats. The queen of turbofolk is Svetlana Ražnatović 'Ceca', the heavy-bosomed wife of the late war criminal and gangster Arkan.

Architecture

Belgrade displays some of the influences of its various historical overlords, minus the Turks' minarets, which were destroyed after independence in 1878. Many of the 19th-century Austro-Hungarian imperial buildings survive, however. Unhappily, far more numerous are the post-WWII buildings, hurriedly erected to meet acute housing needs and bearing the modernist imprint of dull concrete and even duller central planning.

Visual Arts

Art in Serbia and Montenegro has been heavily influenced by European trends, although religious icons stand out as a distinctive national tradition. Art galleries in Belgrade present an eclectic range of art from landscape and figurative to installation pieces and abstract work.

The Albania building: Belgrade's first skyscraper (1940)

The works of the Croatian sculptor Ivan Meštrović (1883–1962) are ubiquitous and you will notice them in several places around Belgrade. Most notable are the Monument to France and Victory Monument in Kalemegdan Citadel (p8) and the Monument to the Unknown Hero in Avala (p20). The Munich-educated impressionist painter Nadežda Petrović (1873–1915) produced some wonderfully energetic portraits. The paintings from her earthy 'Serbian period' (1903–10) show a change in perception from those of her earlier, more impassioned 'Munich period' (1898–1903). Her final and perhaps most accomplished paintings come from the 'Parisian period' (1910–12). Many of her paintings are displayed in Belgrade's National Museum (p17).

Directory

ARRIVAL & DEPARTURE
Air

Serbia and Montenegro is well served by regional airlines that pick up at intercontinental hubs. Travellers from Australasia can fly to Dubai and pick up a JAT flight to Belgrade, or fly with Lufthansa via Frankfurt or Austrian Airlines via Vienna. Travellers from North America can pick up connecting flights in London or Frankfurt. As yet none of the European discount airlines fly to or near Belgrade, although it is feasible to fly into Budapest with easyJet and then take the train to Belgrade. Departure tax for domestic/international flights is 500/1000DIN, although this is usually covered in the price of your ticket.

Belgrade's **Surčin airport** (☎ 601 424/601 431; 🖳 www.airport-belgrade. co.yu) handles the majority of international flights. The following office telephone numbers are in Belgrade (area code ☎ 011).

Aeroflot (airline code SU; ☎ 323 5814; www.aeroflot.com) Hub Moscow Sheremetyevo.

Air France (airline code AF; ☎ 638 378; www.airfrance.com) Hub Paris Charles de Gaulle.

Alitalia (airline code AZ; ☎ 324 5344; www.alitalia.com) Hub Rome.

Austrian Airlines (airline code OS; ☎ 324 8077; www.aua.com) Hub Vienna.

British Airways (airline code BA; ☎ 328 1303; www.britishairways.com) Hub London Heathrow.

ČSA (airline code OK; ☎ 361 4592; www. csa.cz) Hub Prague.

JAT (airline code JU; ☎ 302 4077; www. jat.com) Hub Belgrade.

KLM (airline code KL; ☎ 328 2747; www. klm.com) Hub Amsterdam.

LOT Polish Airlines (airline code LOT; ☎ 324 8892; www.lot.com) Hub Warsaw.

Lufthansa (airline code LH; ☎ 322 4975; www.lufthansa.com) Hub Frankfurt.

Montenegro Airlines (airline code YM; ☎ 262 1122; www.montenegro-airlines. com) Hub Podgorica.

Swiss International Air Lines (airline code LX; ☎ 3030 140; www.swiss.com) Hub Zürich.

AIRPORT ACCESS

Surčin airport is 18km west of Belgrade. The **JAT bus** (3, D6; ☎ 675 583) connects the airport with the Jat bus terminal at **Trg Slavija** (3, D6; 120DIN, 5am-9pm hourly airport–town, 7am-8pm hourly town–airport) and the central train station (3, B5). Ignore the taxi sharks prowling inside the airport terminal; go outside and catch a cab to town for around 600DIN.

Bus

The country is well served by buses. International services run to and from Western Europe as well as Turkey, with daily buses linking a number of cities. Sample routes from Belgrade are Malmö in Sweden (34 hours, Friday), Munich (17 hours, daily), Paris (28 hours, Monday, Tuesday, Thursday and Friday) and Zürich (23 hours, Saturday).

Belgrade has two adjacent bus stations: **BAS** (3, B4; ☎ 636 299; Železnička 4) serves regional Serbia and some destinations in Montenegro, while **Lasta** (3 B4; ☎ 625 740; Železnička bb) covers destinations around Belgrade.

Bas Turist (3, B4; ☎ 638 555; fax 784 859; BAS bus station) Sells international bus tickets.

Lasta ticket office (3, C4; ☎ 641 251; www.lasta.co.yu; Milovana Milovanovića 1; 🕙 7am-9pm) Sells international bus tickets.

Train

All international rail connections out of Serbia originate in Belgrade, with most of those heading north and west calling at Novi Sad and Subotica and those heading east calling at Niš. Nonsensically, tickets for international trains have to be paid for in euros, but sleeper supplements have to be paid for in dinars. Here are some sample services from Belgrade to other European destinations:

Destination	Frequency	Duration
Bucharest	daily	14hr
Budapest	daily	7hr
Istanbul	daily	26hr
Ljubljana	daily	10hr
Moscow	daily	50hr
Munich	daily	17hr
Sofia	daily	11hr
Thessaloniki	daily	16hr
Vienna	daily	11hr
Zagreb	daily	7hr

The **central train station** (3, B5; ☎ 629 400; Savski Trg 2) has an extremely helpful information office (☎ 361 8487; platform 1; ☯ 7am-7pm). There's also a small **tourist office** (☎ 361 2732; ☯ 7am-9.30pm Mon-Sat, 10am-6pm Sun) which can provide basic city information and maps. You'll also find an **exchange bureau** (☯ 6am-10pm) and **sales counter** (☎ /fax 265 8868; ☯ 9am-4pm Mon-Sat) for Eurail passes at the track end of the station.

You can buy your tickets (bus or train) in the city centre at **Putnik Travel Agency** (3, C3) ☎ 334 5619; Trg Nikole Pašića 1; ☯ 8am-8pm Mon-Fri, 9am-3pm Sat) for no extra charge, and your train tickets at station prices without the crowds at **KSR Beograd Tours** (3, C5; ☎ 641 258; fax 687 447; Milovana Milovanovića 5; ☯ 6.30am-8pm).

Travel Documents
PASSPORT
If you need a visa for Serbia (see below), it's a good idea to ensure your passport is valid for several months after the due date of entry.

VISA
Most visitors no longer need a visa for short visits to Serbia. Tourist visas for less than 90 days are not required for citizens of most European countries, Australia, New Zealand, Canada or the USA. The website of the Ministry of Foreign Affairs (www.mfa. gov.yu) has full details.

If you're not staying at a hotel or in a private home you're theoretically supposed to register with the police within 24 hours of arrival and subsequently on changing address, although this requirement may be relaxed in the near future.

Customs & Duty Free
If you're bringing in more than €2000, then you have to complete a currency declaration form on arrival and show it on departure. In practice it's ignored but the reality is that if customs officials wanted to play by the rules they could confiscate your money. Play it safe and declare.

Left Luggage
There's a 24-hour left luggage service at the **central train station** (3, B5; Savski Trg 2; 60DIN per piece per day).

GETTING AROUND
The city centre is compact, so in Old Town walking is usually the easiest way to explore. The rather ancient bus, trolleybus and tram network is extensive if confusing. Taxis are by far the quickest and easiest way to travel longer distances.

Bus & Tram
Belgrade's ramshackle bus, tram and trolleybus network covers the whole city, Novi Beograd and the suburbs. Buses are by far the most common. Tickets for all three modes of transport cost 20DIN from a street kiosk or 30DIN from the driver; make sure you validate the ticket in the machine on board. Tram 2 is useful for

connecting Kalemegdan Citadel with Trg Slavija, bus stations and the central train station.

If you're travelling to an unfamiliar destination, it pays to use a map to keep track of your journey or to consult fellow passengers (many of whom will be able and willing to assist in English) since much of the network is signposted only in the Cyrillic alphabet.

Bicycle

Belgrade is hilly and the cars clogging its streets belch fumes. Unsurprisingly there are not many cyclists here and road-users are not cycle savvy, so cycling is unlikely to be enjoyable. The best place to stretch those cycling muscles is along Ada Ciganlija's flat, traffic-free pathways. There are several hire places near the lake (p15).

Taxi

Belgrade's taxis are plentiful and most use meters. Flag fall is 35DIN to 45DIN (depending on the company) and a 5km trip should cost around 200DIN. If the meter's not running, then point it out to the driver. Taxi sharks, usually in flash cars, prey around the airport and outside train and bus stations looking for a rich fare. Airport to city should be about 600DIN; at the stations move away from the entrance and pick up a cruising cab. Have your hotel call you a taxi or phone **Maxis** (☎ 581 111) or **Plavi** (☎ 555 999).

Car & Motorcycle

As in any big city, parking in Belgrade is not always easy to find. Belgraders park on the pavements. It's even regulated, with three parking zones requiring tickets bought from a street kiosk.

ROAD RULES

Cars in Serbia and Montenegro have left-hand drive, seat belts must be worn and the blood-alcohol limit is 0.05%. Traffic police

are everywhere, so drive carefully and stick to speed limits: 120km/h on motorways, 100km/h on dual carriageways, 80km/h on main roads and 60km/h in urban areas. In the event of an accident, the **traffic police** (☎ 92) should be called.

RENTAL

There are plenty of hire companies. **VIP** (☎ 690 107), **Hertz** (☎ 600 634) and **Europcar** (☎ 601 555) all have offices at Belgrade's Surčin airport. The typical cost of small-car hire in Serbia is €45 a day.

DRIVING LICENCE & PERMIT

Drivers without an EU licence should obtain an International Driving Permit. Vehicles need Green Card insurance (costing around €80 per month), if this is not already covered by a car hire agreement.

MOTORING ORGANISATIONS

The **Auto-Moto Savez Serbia & Montenegro** (Serbia & Montenegro Automotive Association; ☎ 011 9800; www.amsj.co.yu; Ruzveltova 18, Belgrade) offers breakdown services. Its website has details of road conditions, tolls, insurance and petrol prices.

PRACTICALITIES
Climate & When to Go

Northern Serbia has a continental climate, with cold winters and hot, humid summers. The best time to visit is during early summer, in May or June. Autumn, from September to October, is also generally warm and pleasant.

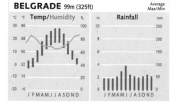

Consulates & Embassies
Australia (☎ 02-6290 2630; yuembau@
ozemail.com.au; 4 Bulwarra Close,
O'Malley, ACT 2606)
Canada (☎ 613 233 6289; www.embscg.
ca/consular.html; 17 Blackburn Ave,
Ottawa, Ontario, K1A 8A2)
UK (☎ 0207-235 9049; www.
yugoslavembassy.org,uk; 28 Belgrave Sq,
London SW1X 8QB)
USA (☎ 202-332 0333; www.yuembusa.
org; 2134 Kalorama Road NW, Washington
DC, 20008)

The following countries have
representation in Belgrade:
Australia (3, C3; ☎ 330 3400; Čika
Ljubina 13)
Canada (3, B6; ☎ 306 3000; Kneza
Miloša 75)
France (3, B2; ☎ 302 3500; Pariska 11)
Germany (3, B6; ☎ 306 4300; Kneza
Miloša 74-6)
UK (3, C6; ☎ 264 5055; Resavska 46)
USA (3, C6; ☎ 361 9344; Kneza Miloša 50)

Disabled Travellers
Disabled travellers are not well catered for as
a general rule. Belgrade does not go out of its
way to make life easy for wheelchair users.

Discounts
The **EURO<26 discount card** (www.
euro26.org.yu) can provide holders with
discounts on rail travel, air travel with JAT
and Montenegro Airlines, and selected
hotels. The **Youth Hostel organisation**
(Ferijalni Savez Beograd; ☎ 324 8550;
www.hostels.org.yu; 2nd fl, Makedonska
22; ☯ 9am-5pm) does discount deals
with local hotels. You need HI (Hostelling
International) membership (300DIN to join)
or an international student card.

Electricity
Serbia and Montenegro uses standard
European voltage (220–240V/50–60Hz).

Emergencies
Ambulance ☎ 94
Fire service ☎ 93
Motoring assistance in Belgrade
☎ 987
Motoring assistance outside Belgrade
☎ 011 9800
Police ☎ 92

Fitness
You're in the wrong city in the wrong
country. The average Belgrader's idea
of exercise is a trip to the tobacconist's,
preferably by public transport. There are a
few options, however.

There's some great running and
walking space along the Danube and
around **Park Prijateljska** (p21) over the
Sava in Novi Beograd. There's the **25 Maj
sports centre** (2, C1; ☎ 622 866) and
public swimming pool beside the Danube
in Dorćol. In summer **Ada Ciganlija**
(p15) offers a delightful environment for
swimming, running or cycling. There's
a very plush gym and spa at the Hyatt
Regency (p43), with a good gym and
swimming pool.

Gay & Lesbian Travellers
Homosexuality has been legal in
Yugoslavia since 1932, and in Serbia, the
age of consent for male-male sex is 18
and for female-female sex 14. However,
significant homophobia has meant that
gay and lesbian residents don't feel
confident in publicly expressing their
sexuality. As a result, events and meeting
places (see p38) are few and the scene is
rather muted and virtually underground.
For more information check www.gay
-serbia.com.

PRECAUTIONS
Belgrade is generally a healthy and disease-
free place. As foreign visitors cannot use
Serbia's health service, health insurance is
recommended.

MEDICAL SERVICES
Boris Kidrič Hospital Diplomatic Section (2, D5; ☎ 643 839; Miloša Porcerca Pasterova 1; ⊙ 7am-7pm Mon-Fri)
Klinički Centar (2, C4; ☎ 361 8444; Miloša Porcerca Pasterova 2; ⊙ 24hr)

PHARMACIES
Prima 1 (3, C5; ☎ 361 0999; Nemanjina 2; ⊙ 24hr)

Holidays
Public holidays in Serbia and Montenegro include:

New Year	1 January
Orthodox Christmas	7 January
Nation Day	27 April
International Labour Days	1 and 2 May
Victory Day	9 May
Republic Day	29 Nov

Orthodox churches celebrate Easter between one and five weeks later than other churches.

Internet
There are several Internet cafés in central Belgrade. A handful of the better hotels also have fast Internet connections, and even wireless connectivity. Beyond these, connecting a laptop to the Internet can be a headache.

INTERNET CAFÉS
Sport Café (3, C3; ☎ 323 3344; off Makedonska 4; per hr 90DIN; ⊙ 9am-midnight Mon-Sat, 11am-1am Sun)
Plato Cyber Club (3, C2; ☎ 635 363; Vase Čarapića 19; per hr 65DIN; ⊙ 9am-11pm)

USEFUL WEBSITES
Lonely Planet's website (www.lonelyplanet. com) offers further information.
Expat Foundation (www.expat.org.uk)

Belgrade City site (www.beograd.org.yu)
Belgrade Airport (www.airport-belgrade.co.yu)
Belgrade Sightseeing (http://solair.eunet.yu/~rabotic
Serbian Government (www.srbija.sr.gov.yu)
Serbian Tourist Organisation (www.serbia-tourism.org)
Tourist Organisation of Belgrade (www.belgradetourism.org.yu)

Metric System
The system used for weights and measurements is metric.

TEMPERATURE
$°C = (°F - 32) ÷ 1.8$
$°F = (°C \times 1.8) + 32$

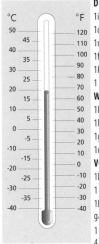

DISTANCE
1in = 2.54cm
1cm = 0.39in
1m = 3.3ft = 1.1yd
1ft = 0.3m
1km = 0.62 miles
1 mile = 1.6km

WEIGHT
1kg = 2.2lb
1lb = 0.45kg
1g = 0.04oz
1oz = 28g

VOLUME
1L= 0.26 US gallons
1 US gallon = 3.8L
1L = 0.22 imperial gallons
1 imperial gallon = 4.55L

Money
ATMs
You won't be stuck for cash on the streets of Belgrade. Some Belgrade banks are installing 24-hour machines for changing foreign notes. There's an ATM at Belgrade's airport that accepts most international cards.

CURRENCY

Unlike Montenegro and Kosovo, which use the euro, Serbia retains the dinar, although some hotels may request payment in euros. Quite a few shops and taxi drivers will accept payment in euros. Some international train journeys may require part payment in dinars and part in euros.

CREDIT CARDS

MasterCard, Visa and Diners Club are widely accepted by businesses.

CHANGING & TRANSFERRING MONEY

A large number of banks cash hard currency travellers cheques; the euro is preferable. Western Union (www .westernunion.com) transfers can be made at most banks and major post offices. The euro is the favoured hard currency. Many exchange offices in Serbia will readily change euros and other hard currencies into dinars and back again when you leave. Look for their large blue diamond signs hanging outside.

Atlas Bank (3, D3; ☎ 302 4000; Emilijana Joksimovića 4; ❧ 8am-5pm Mon-Fri, 8am-1pm Sat) Cashes travellers cheques.

Delta Banka (3, C3; ☎ 302 2624; Knez Mihailova 30; ❧ 6.30am-10pm) Has an ATM and cashes travellers cheques.

EXCHANGE RATES

For current exchange rates see www.oanda.com.

Australia	A$1	74DIN
Canada	C$1	65DIN
Euro zone	€1	88DIN
Hungary	100Ft	35DIN
Japan	¥100	64DIN
New Zealand	NZ$1	49DIN
UK	£1	129DIN
USA	US$1	74DIN

Newspapers & Magazines

Danas and *Politika* are daily newspapers, and *Vreme* and *NIN* weekly magazines. *Yellowcab* (www.yellowcab.co.yu), a widely available local monthly listings magazine for Belgrade, has some information in English. Several newsagents and newsstands around the city sell international newspapers and magazines.

Opening Hours

Banks in Belgrade keep very long hours, often 7am to 7pm weekdays and 7am to noon Saturday. On weekdays many shops open at 8am and close at 6pm. Department stores, supermarkets and some restaurants and bars are open all day. Most government offices close on Saturday. Although shops stay open on Saturday until 2pm, many other businesses close at 3pm.

Photography & Video

Check with the police before photographing any official building they're guarding. Some of the bombed-out buildings just outside the city centre were, and officially still are, military premises. It's advisable to ask permission before you take photos at these locations.

Post

Parcels should be taken unsealed to the main post office for inspection. Allow time to check the post office's repacking and complete the transaction. You can receive mail, addressed poste restante, for a small charge.

Central Post Office (3, C3; ☎ 633 492; Takovska 2; ❧ 8am-7pm Mon-Sat)

Radio

The state national broadcaster is RTS, but, in recent years, a plethora of new, small independent radio stations have sprung up, many of them aimed at Belgrade's youth and playing a vibrant mix of contemporary music. B92 radio is the main independent broadcaster.

Telephone

Payphones are easy to find in the city centre, and the majority require a phonecard, which may be purchased at newsstands. On Serbian and Montenegrin public phones, press the 'i' button for dialling commands in English. Some businesses do not have land-line telephones but can be contacted via mobile phone whose numbers usually start with 06 or 04.

INTERNATIONAL CALLS

Some hotels are not set up to offer overseas phone calls, nor for that matter, calls to local mobile numbers. In the older communist-era hotels forget trying to get an internet connection on your laptop through the phone system. Phonecards are widely available for local calls but don't give enough time for an international call, so use telephone centres at post offices. Alternatively, some of the central internet cafés now offer headsets for voice-over-internet calls with services such as Skype.

Telephone centre (3, C3; ☎ 323 4484; Takovska 2, Central Post Office; ☽ 7am-midnight Mon-Fri, 7am-10pm Sat & Sun)

MOBILE PHONES

Mobile phone users with GSM, dual- or tri-band phones and the right roaming contract with their home provider should have no problems taking calls. For making local calls it's also quite feasible and cost-effective to buy and use a local SIM card; just make sure your home network has not locked your handset to its own SIM cards. Local SIM cards are available from the many mobile phone vendors in town.

COUNTRY & CITY CODES

Belgrade country code ☎ 381
International access code ☎ 99

Television

RTS is the state national broadcaster but there are several private competitors. Needless to say, these channels are in Serbian only and the output can be pretty dismal (a couple of hours of turbofolk videos followed by a tarot card reading phone-in anyone?). Most hotels in town have cable or satellite and provide the main news channels from around Europe and beyond, including BBC World and CNN.

Tipping

Apart from in Belgrade's smarter restaurants, tipping is not generally expected. Rounding up the bill at cafés and adding 10% in the better restaurants is fine. Belgraders do not generally tip taxi drivers.

Tourist Information

Belgrade's tourist organisation is helpful and, although its resources are somewhat limited, things are improving all the time. Its information centres have plenty of maps and brochures to hand out and their English-speaking staff are knowledgeable.

Tourist Organisation of Belgrade
(3, C3; ☎ 629 992; Knez Mihailova 18;
☽ 9am 8pm Mon-Fri, 9am-6pm Sat,
11am-5pm Sun)
Terazije Underpass (3, C3; ☎ 635 622;
☽ 9am-8pm Mon-Fri, 9am-4pm Sat)

Women Travellers

Other than a cursory interest shown by men towards solo women travellers, travelling is generally hassle-free and easy. In Muslim areas a few women wear a headscarf but most young women adopt Western fashions.

LANGUAGE

Serbian is by far the most common language in Serbia. Many Serbs also know some English, German and Russian and young Serbs in particular are often virtually fluent in English. Serbian is a Slavic language closely related to Russian, Czech and Polish, and with many Turkish influences.

PRONUNCIATION

Serbian uses both the Cyrillic and Roman alphabet. When written in the Roman alphabet, many letters are pronounced as in English. The following outlines some pronunciations that are specific to Serbian.

c	as the 'ts' in 'cats'
ć	as the 'tu' in 'future'
č	as the 'ch' in 'chop'
đ	as the 'j' in 'jury'
dž	as the 'dj' in 'adjust'
j	as the 'y' in 'young'
lj	as the 'lli' in 'million'
nj	as the 'ny' in 'canyon'
š	as the 'sh' in 'hush'
ž	as the 's' in 'pleasure'

BASICS

Hello.	Zdravo.
Goodbye.	Doviđenja.
How are you?	Kako ste?
Yes.	Da.
No.	Ne.
Please.	Molim.
Thank you.	Hvala.
You're welcome.	Nema na čemu.
Excuse me.	Izvinite.
Sorry.	Žao mi je.
May I?	Da li mogu?
My name is ...	Zovem se ...
I'm from ...	Ja sam iz ...

ACCOMMODATION

I'm looking for a ...	Tražim ...
guesthouse	pansion
hotel	hotel

Do you have any rooms available?	Imate li slobodnih soba?
I'd like (a) ... single room	Hteo/Htela bih ... (m/f) jednokrevetnu sobu
double/twin bedroom room with a bathroom	dvokrevetnu sobu sobu sa kupatilom
How much is it ...? per night per person	Koliko košta ...? za noć po osobi

DIRECTIONS

Where is ...?	Gde je ...?
Go straight ahead.	Idite pravo napred.
Turn left.	Skrenite levo.
Turn right.	Skrenite desno.

EMERGENCIES

Help!	Upomoć!
There's been an accident!	Desila se nezgoda!
I'm lost.	Izgubio/Izgubila sam se. (m/f)
I'm ill.	Ja sam bolestan/ bolesna. (m/f)
Call a doctor!	Zovite lekara.
Call the police!	Zovite policiju.

EATING

I'm a vegetarian.	Ja sam vegetarijanac/ vegetarijanka. (m/f)
Waiter!	Konobar!
What would you recommend?	Šta biste nam preporučili?
Please bring the bill.	Molim vas donesite račun.
breakfast	doručak
lunch	ručak
dinner	večera

LANGUAGE DIFFICULTIES

Do you speak (English)?	Govorite/Govoriš li (engleski)? polite/informal
I (don't) understand.	Ja (ne) razumem.
Can you show me (on the map)?	Možete li to da mi pokažete (na karti)?

NUMBERS

1	jedan
2	dva
3	tri
4	četiri
5	pet
6	šest
7	sedam
8	osam
9	devet
10	deset
100	sto
1000	hiljadu

SHOPPING & SERVICES

I'm just looking.	Ja samo razgledam.
I'd like to buy (an adaptor plug).	Želim da kupim (utikač za adapter).
May I look at it?	Mogu li to da pogledam?
How much is it?	Koliko košta?
I like it.	Sviđa mi se.
I'll take it.	Uzeću ovo.
Where do I pay?	Gde se plaća?
Do you accept ...?	Da li prihvatate ...?
credit cards	kreditne kartice
travellers cheques	putničke čekove
Where's ...	Gde je ...?
a bank	banka
the hospital	bolnica
the market	pijaca
a public toilet	javni toalet
a supermarket	samoposluga
the tourist office	turistički biro

TIME & DATES

What time is it?	Koliko je sati?
It's (one) o'clock.	(Jedan) je sat.
It's (10) o'clock.	(Deset) je sat.
in the morning	ujutro
in the afternoon	poslepodne
in the evening	uveče
today	danas
tomorrow	sutra
yesterday	juče
Monday	ponedeljak
Tuesday	utorak
Wednesday	sreda
Thursday	četvrtak
Friday	petak
Saturday	subota
Sunday	nedelja
January	januar
February	februar
March	mart
April	april
May	maj
June	juni
July	juli
August	avgust
September	septembar
October	oktobar
November	novembar
December	decembar

TRANSPORT

What time does the ... leave/arrive?	U koliko sati kreće/ stiže ...?
boat	brod
bus	autobus
plane	avion
train	voz
tram	tramvaj
I'd like a ... ticket.	Hteo/Htela bih jednu ... kartu. (m/f)
one-way	jednosmernu
return	povratnu
I want to go to ...	Želim da idem u ...

Index

FEATURES

- Pekara Centar Pizza............... *Eating*
- Tuckwood Cineplex........ *Entertainment*
- Monin Bar........................... *Drinking*
- Nikola Tesla Museum......... *Highlights*
- Millennium Centre................ *Shopping*
- Gallery of Frescoes...... *Sights/Activities*
- Hotel Zlatnik....................... *Sleeping*
- Novi Sad.................... *Trips & Tours*

AREAS

- ....Beach, Desert
- ....Building
- ....Land
- ....Mall
- ....Market
- ....Other Area
- ....Park/Cemetery
- ....Sports
- ....Urban

HYDROGRAPHY

- ....River, Creek
- ....Intermittent River
- ....Water

BOUNDARIES

- ....International
- ....State, Provincial
- ....Regional, Suburb
- ....Ancient Wall

ROUTES

- ....Tollway
- ....Freeway
- ....Primary Road
- ....Secondary Road
- ....Tertiary Road
- ....Lane
- ....Under Construction
- ....One-Way Street
- ....Unsealed Road
- ....Mall/Steps
- ....Tunnel
- ....Walking Path
- ....Walking Trail/Track
- ....Pedestrian Overpass
- ....Walking Tour

TRANSPORT

- ....Airport, Airfield
- ....Bus Route
- ....Cycling, Bicycle Path
- ....Ferry
- ....General Transport
- ....Metro
- ....Monorail
- ....Rail
- ....Taxi Rank
- ....Tram

SYMBOLS

- ....Bank, ATM
- ....Buddhist
- ....Castle, Fortress
- ....Christian
- ....Diving, Snorkeling
- ....Embassy, Consulate
- ....Hospital, Clinic
- ....Information
- ....Internet Access
- ....Islamic
- ....Jewish
- ....Lighthouse
- ....Lookout
- ....Monument
- ....Mountain, Volcano
- ....National Park
- ....Parking Area
- ....Petrol Station
- ....Picnic Area
- ....Point of Interest
- ....Police Station
- ....Post Office
- ....Ruin
- ....Telephone
- ....Toilets
- ....Zoo, Bird Sanctuary
- ....Waterfall